With Open Arms
Short Stories of
Misadventures in Morocco

Matthew Félix

With Open Arms:
Short Stories of Misadventures in Morocco
by Matthew Félix

Published by sⵣificatio

2016 Trade Paperback Edition

matthewfelix.com

Cover Photo Credits:
Detail of "Puerta del palacio real"
Copyright 2009 by Pau Link
Photo: http://bit.ly/1MtnL9m
License: http://bit.ly/1jxQJMa

ISBN-10: 0-9977619-0-3
ISBN-13: 978-0-9977619-0-0

CONTENTS

1 TIME TO GO BACK

After nearly three months in Europe visiting friends and working on some writing projects, the time came to renew my tourist visa. The process was easy: I just had to leave the European Union and come back in. Simple. There was no paperwork nor any other sort of bureaucracy with which to contend. And the choice for my point of exit was obvious.

I was going to Morocco.

Having settled temporarily in southern Spain, all I needed to do was take a bus to the port of Algeciras, where I could catch one of the many ferries that traverse the Straight of Gibraltar each day. The trip wouldn't take long, only nine miles separating the Iberian Peninsula from Africa at their closest point.

I had been to Morocco before. Consequently, despite how easy obtaining my visa would be in theory, I knew the reality could prove another thing altogether. A familiar anxiety from the past had already taken hold of me, like a concerned loved one sitting me down to make me question what the hell I was thinking. I have done a fair amount of traveling and, of all the countries I've visited, none was more challenging than Morocco.

Did I really want to go back?

Four or five years had passed since my first visit. The knot in my stomach notwithstanding, a part of me couldn't stand the thought of being so close without returning, even if only for a few days. My curiosity got the better of my fears, and soon I was planning my trip.

Despite the stories I'm about to tell, I don't regret my decision. Neither, for that matter, have I ever or would I discourage anyone else from visiting Morocco. I've met plenty of travelers, after all, who fared much better than I, travelers whose positive experiences far outweighed any complaints they might have had about overeager medina merchants. Consequently, even given my own experiences, I can't say I'll never go back.

Perhaps third time's the charm.

2 WELCOME TO TANGIER

The guidebook I had on my first trip provided lengthy warnings of what to expect upon arriving in Tangier. Still, nothing could have prepared me for the welcoming I was about to receive as I stepped off the boat. Perhaps I should have paid closer attention to the literal plank we had to walk to disembark. But by then it was too late.

I looked up from where my feet had landed and discovered a throng of locals waiting outside the dock. It was a nightmarish scene, and my entire body tensed in dreaded anticipation of the gauntlet I was about to run. I looked around for another way out, only to confirm my fears. Unless I wanted to swim through the shark-infested waters back to Spain, I had to resign myself to my fate, each step heavier than the last for reasons that had nothing to do with the weight of my backpack.

As though my time had come to repay a long-forgotten karmic debt, I threw myself into the lynch mob, walking as quickly as possible without making eye contact with any of my would-be assailants. It didn't matter. Like a celebrity smothered by paparazzi, I was assaulted on all sides by an overwhelming barrage of unsolicited questions and insistent offers. All I could do was try to keep walking, which was no easy task.

"Welcome friend!" said a man whose particularly aggressive tactics had somehow distinguished him from the rest of the crowd. Tall, dark, and greasy, with beady eyes, a long, hooked nose, and a face that hadn't been shaved for days, he had obviously laid claim to me. All the other men fell back like children conceding victory to a departing train.

"*¿Español?*"

Hoping to walk the extremely fine line between neither encouraging nor offending him, without saying a word I smiled half-heartedly and kept going.

"Where are you from?" the man attempted again, innocently, as though he harbored a secret hope we might someday be friends.

When I still showed no sign of engaging, he ventured, "*Vous êtes Français?*" There were, after all, only so many possibilities. He was going to go through each and every one until he stumbled upon the nationality that made my eyes light up.

In spite of myself, a "no" slipped out. That was all. Nothing more. I couldn't help it. It was too hard to ignore someone—his motives notwithstanding—staring me right in the face. Besides, it was hardly an invitation to conversation. I hoped he would get the hint and give it a rest.

But an invitation is exactly what my self-appointed host heard in my monosyllabic utterance. Whether I realized it or not, he had just got his foot in the door, and he wasn't about to waste any time before forcing himself inside.

"English! Are you English! American?" he asked, with relief bordering on elation now that things were starting to go his way.

I kept walking, once again falling mute, hating myself for having given in.

"Is this your first time in Morocco?"

I didn't know what to do. He was looming over me, encroaching so completely on my personal space that even my shadow was crowded out. His face was so close I could smell whatever was festering in his gut, and his eyes were opened so wide all I could see were my own reflected back. There was no way to ignore him. It was only a matter of time before the pressure became too much, my manners again subjugating my sense of self-preservation.

"Yes," I replied as dispassionately as possible, still naively clinging to the hope he would pick up on my disinterest and leave me alone.

Having already made two big mistakes, I had now made an even bigger one. I never should have admitted it was my first time in Morocco. I may as well have added, "And since you were kind enough to ask, no one knows I'm here, I have no idea where I'm going, and I don't have a clue how much anything costs."

"Ah, wonderful! Welcome! I will take you to a very nice hotel," the man said rather than asked, suddenly distracted as though counting the piles of money destined to be his as the result of our fortuitous encounter. All the while, he kept in flawless lockstep with me as we left the port behind and began the steep climb towards the narrow, labyrinthine alleys of the old town, or medina, imposing overhead.

Under ordinary circumstances, it would have been challenging enough. I didn't know where I was going, and the medina, its layout lacking any apparent logic, was sure to be difficult to negotiate for a newcomer. But these weren't ordinary circumstances. Dusk was fast approaching, and my unwanted companion's persistence flirted dangerously with belligerence. I decided to return to my initial tactic of saying nothing.

If the two words I had said up until then had been misconstrued as gestures of goodwill, my return to silence was taken as a declaration of war.

"Why do you act this way!" the man demanded, frustrated our budding friendship, which only moments before he had been convinced was on the verge of blossoming—not to mention bearing fruit—was suddenly threatened by the icy chill of my cold shoulder.

I held my ground and said nothing.

"Why are you so paranoid!" he pressed, raising both the pitch and volume of his voice.

I now understood both sides of the game. If I so much as grunted, it was an open invitation to conversation. As long as he had me talking, the man figured he could eventually wear me down. If, on the other hand, I said nothing, he would take offense and try to either guilt or scare me into re-engaging. It was a no-win situation, and he had deliberately set it up that way.

"Are you racist?"

Unconvincing in his role as guardian angel—and his time, like mine, quickly running out—he had given up on the charade. His true colors now shined through.

Again I said nothing, my attention diverted to an almost more daunting concern: somehow getting my bearings amidst the anarchy that opened up before me, a pit in my stomach opening up right along with it.

We had arrived at the main plaza of the medina, a chaotic crossroads. Hoards of people came and went up and down unmarked alleys spinning off in all directions like twisted spokes of a wheel. Signs posted wherever the eye could see created more confusion than they gave direction, frustrating my frantic struggle to reconcile what I now saw with the map I'd committed to memory before getting off the boat. The chances of navigating the insanity on my own were next to nil.

And that was exactly what the man was counting on.

"You must be Jewish, otherwise you wouldn't act this way!" he sneered, oblivious to the irony of following up his previous comment with this one.

I was at my wits' end. Before I even knew what I was doing, I dove into a tiny shop facing the plaza, a desperate, spontaneous move to throw the man off my trail.

To my complete surprise, it worked.

"Excusez-moi," I beseeched, praying that the man standing before the floor-to-ceiling wall of reams and reams of colorful fabrics would be sympathetic. *"Je cherche l'Hôtel Meknès."*

The man said nothing. Instead, he smiled calmly, walked

around the old wooden display case that had separated us until then, and took me by the arm back outside. Still smiling, he gestured for me to look up. The Hotel Meknes was right there, just across the little plaza. I had made it without realizing it, since in my confusion it hadn't occurred to me that the first floor of the hotel might not be located at street level. Even the sign was higher than I was likely to look, given all the others closer to the ground competing with it for attention.

Immensely relieved, I thanked the man profusely. Without saying a word, he smiled again and made his way back inside.

Once more on my own, I looked around anxiously, reassured to find that my escort from the port was nowhere in sight. The hotel entrance was out of sight, too, in an alley just off the plaza. The coast now clear, I headed towards it, praying there would be a room available.

The welcome end of my journey nearly within reach—the relief of a cool shower, the security of a door locked behind me, the luxury of a large bed in which to stretch out my weary limbs—I stepped into the doorway, hesitating when I saw it was very poorly lit.

No sooner had I done so, than a man lunged at me from the darkness.

"What are you doing here!" he demanded in French.

I reeled backwards. The nightmare, it was instantly clear, was far from over.

"I'm sorry, ah—" I didn't know what to say. Was I trespassing? Wasn't this the entrance to the hotel? I looked up. The sign was there. I was in the right place.

"What do you want!" growled the man, inching closer, like a cougar about to pounce. Throwing his head back, he stuck his chest out in an even more threatening display of aggression.

"I'm here for a room—I'm going to the hotel," I offered, my French a muddled mess given my shock.

"There aren't any rooms! The hotel is full!" the thug insisted, relaxing ever so slightly as he took satisfied note of my confusion.

I had heard that line before; actually, I had read it. The

guidebook warned of con men who lied about one hotel being full, so they could whisk their unsuspecting victims off to another that would pay a commission for customers delivered to their doorstep. This guy was obviously one of them. He was trying to make me feel I had done something wrong, so he could then ease up, make friends, and offer to take me to another place that—as luck would have it—did have some rooms available. Still, being onto his ploy didn't make him any less of a threat.

I looked up the staircase leading to the hotel lobby, out of sight somewhere above. This man was smaller than the first, but my mobility was restricted by a large backpack. I would hardly be able to defend myself if it came to that. On the other hand, we were just off a plaza full of people, and there should be more at the top of the stairs. Someone was sure to hear if I called for help. Weren't they? Regardless, I resented being put in the situation—especially so soon after the first one, from which I hadn't even had a chance to recover—and I didn't want to give into more lies and intimidation.

So I decided to play dumb.

Unknowingly using a ploy that more than one cabdriver would later try on me, I suddenly forgot how to speak French. It helped that I hadn't done so very well initially. When the man said something else, I just looked at him even more confused. Tilting my head as though I hadn't understood, I responded in Spanish, "No rooms, really?"

Thank god he hardly spoke Spanish.

Thrown by the unexpected change to the rules of engagement, the sinister expression the man had exhibited until then gave way to a genuinely perplexed one. He was now the one scratching his head, trying to figure out what was going on and how the tide had changed. I then knew for sure we were in fact playing a game.

"No...uh, hotel full. Ah...no rooms!" He spoke louder than before, impulsively falling victim to that erroneous yet timeless notion that a language divide can be bridged by yelling across it.

Although I no longer appeared to understand him nearly as well as I had mere moments before, I nodded vaguely as though some of what he said registered. Still, pretending not to get how definite he was, I flashed as confident and convincing a smile as I could muster and told him I was going upstairs to double-check—just to be sure.

"No, there is..." he began, visibly confused and increasingly frustrated, as he felt me wiggling free of his grasp.

"Just to be sure..." I repeated with another smile, turning to begin the ascent—and praying I wasn't miscalculating.

The stairs rose indifferently before me, quickly rounding a corner that—I hoped—concealed the hotel entrance. From the outside the hotel appeared to start on the second floor; but, I didn't actually know for sure. A burnt-out light bulb overhead dangled from a frayed cord, a few cockroaches lay at my feet, their legs forever upturned in petrified agony, and a potential attacker debated his next move at my back. My heart was pounding, and I was covered in sweat. Still, trusting that the end to my nightmarish introduction to Morocco was a mere flight or two away, I started climbing.

Was the thug following me? Was I a fool for letting down my defenses? Or had I called his bluff? What if I got to the lobby and the hotel really was full? What was I going to do then? "It won't be. It won't be," I reassured myself, refusing to be had by the second belligerent con artist I'd encountered in less than an hour in the country.

Three quarters of the way up the first flight of stairs no one had attacked me from behind. I rounded the corner, proceeded up another half-flight, and discovered what I had desperately hoped to find: a hotel lobby.

The reception area was dim and musty, with a pungent odor of stale tobacco. It didn't matter. Beaming as I was on the inside, the entire lobby may as well have been aglow in a heavenly light. I didn't even need to see my room. I was home.

Getting up from his seat amongst a group of young men watching a soccer match, a friendly older gentleman checked me in and showed me to my room. It was simple and run down, with no bathroom. At least it had a sink with running water, and it was large and more or less clean. It also had the charm of high ceilings with decorative moldings that recalled better days, as well as two sets of French doors. Each set opened onto its own small balcony overlooking the plaza.

Standing on one of the balconies, I contemplated Tangier for the first time. Directly below, as well as kitty-corner to my hotel, men sat at outdoor cafés, conversing over cups of coffee and glasses of mint tea. Interspersed with the locals, I spied a few tourists, including a Danish couple I recognized from the ferry trip over. There were all sorts of small shops—the fabric store in plain sight—several food vendors, and never-ending streams of people coming and going in all directions. Men for the most part, some were dressed in traditional robe-like garments and pointy leather shoes, whereas others wore t-shirts or button-downs and blue jeans or slacks. Food was being cooked with unfamiliar yet enticing spices, cigarettes were going up in smoke faster than kindling on a bonfire, and a saltiness on the air recalled the proximity to the sea.

Too exhausted to take in any more, I closed the shutters, left one of the French doors cracked to let in some air, and pulled down the sheets. Collapsing as though finally succumbing to the weight of the trials and tribulations I'd endured on my odyssey from the port, at long last I was able to savor the fact I had made it. Having been hassled, lied to, insulted, and threatened, I was safe and sound in my own hotel room.

Despite the unrelenting buzz of activity outside and the sporadic outbursts of the young men in the lobby, my eyelids were soon struggling against the same weight that had knocked me off my feet moments before. I heard the frenzied cheers when one of the soccer teams scored a goal, but by the time they died back down I had already fallen into one of the deepest slumbers of my life.

It was a good thing, too. I would need to be as fully rested as possible for what was to come.

3 TWO BUS RIDES TO FEZ

Memories of my previous trip at the forefront of my mind, I had done it: I'd gotten on another ferry to Morocco. This time, however, I wasn't alone.

As we made the crossing, I told my French friend Sophie about my first arrival in Tangier, sparing her too many details for fear of overwhelming her before we even got off the boat. I wanted her not only to be prepared for any difficulties we might face, but also to understand why in certain situations I might react in ways that could seem insensitive or even rude.

The most important rule of thumb was to not trust anyone who approached us. Not a frail, hunched-over 90-year-old woman. Not an innocent, adorable child flashing the brightest of smiles. No one. As harsh as it might sound, on my first trip the need for such an extreme approach had been driven home over and over again. To illustrate why, I shared with Sophie my experience on a bus from Chefchaouen to Fez.

A couple of hours into the trip, the rugged altitudes of the Rif mountains having given way to barren desert, we came to a belabored stop. Through the stream of passengers hustling off the stuffy bus and into the blinding sun, I saw a rest stop of sorts. I still had pistachios I'd bought in Chefchaouen, as well as cookies and some water. Stretching my legs would have been nice, but I didn't actually need anything. Since neither did I want to risk losing my seat, I decided to stay put.

Splitting apart one pistachio after another, I observed the activity outside. People returning from the bathroom, noticeably more relaxed now that the pressure was off. A vendor selling snacks and drinks, scrambling to tend to everyone's needs during the brief interval the bus was at rest. Some passengers animated and visibly relieved to move around; others scarcely moving a muscle, languishing in the heat as though regretting having gotten off the bus at all.

As I opened my water and took a long drink, I had the impression I was being watched. Turning slightly over my shoulder, mere inches away I discovered a well-kempt, middle-aged Moroccan man eagerly smiling at me.

"Français?" he asked without missing a beat.

"Non," I responded with a smile, returning to my pistachios.

It was maddening. Over and over again I had been asked my nationality, each time as precursor to a long list of questions intended to determine what goods and services might be forced upon me.

"Belge? Canadien?"

It didn't matter that I was no longer facing his direction. The man had no qualms about talking to the back of my head. What's more, we were on a bus. I wasn't going anywhere, and neither was he. There was no way of politely ignoring him.

"Je suis Americain," I responded, once again trying to convey as much disinterest as possible without being altogether rude.

"Ah! American! What city are you from? I have a brother who is a doctor in Los Angeles!"

The guy seemed innocent enough, and I wondered if he was actually telling the truth. I decided to see how much he knew about Los Angeles.

"I'm from San Francisco, but I have friends in L.A. Have you ever been?"

"Oh no, I've never been able to go. I live in France, so I only see my brother once a year for family events. That's why

I'm here now. I was on my way to my sister's wedding, but my car broke down, so I had to get on the bus a few towns back."

"How horrible! I'm really sorry to hear that."

I suspected the con had begun, but I wasn't sure. The man did speak French well enough to actually live in France, and he appeared to have financial means consistent with his story, given his clothes, grooming, and expensive-looking watch. He hadn't asked for anything, so maybe I was just being paranoid.

"Yes, it was very bad, but at least the bus came not too long after, so it's okay. You know, since you are going to Fez I invite you to come to my sister's wedding. It is going to be wonderful, and I can tell that you are a nice guy. It would be a great opportunity for you to see a traditional Berber wedding, and you could stay with my family. Yes, you are an American, so that would be good."

I wondered what being American had to do with being a good guest at a Berber wedding, but decided not to ask.

"Thank you very much—that's really kind of you to offer. But I couldn't impose on a family event like that."

"No, no, no! It's no problem! This is Morocco, and we love to receive guests and share our culture. We would be honored to have you be there. Of course, if you don't think it sounds nice or don't want to come..." His voice trailed off, pained as though the very thought I might refuse his invitation were more than he could bear.

In fact it did sound nice, and I was very interested. This was why I had come to Morocco: to get to know the people and the culture. What the man was describing seemed like an incredible opportunity. I was reluctant to turn it down simply because my previous experiences had made me too cynical to trust anyone I met on the road. On the other hand, what if he was just another con artist—one who had developed a more sophisticated and believable scam than the others I had already encountered? It seemed far-fetched, but it was possible.

"When is it?" I asked. "You see, I'm meeting some people in Fez..."

I wasn't meeting anyone in Fez, but I felt like I needed an

out to play it safe. In the event the man was sincere but I decided not to go, hopefully it would also reduce the risk of offending him.

"It's tonight. That's why I think it would be very easy for you, if you wanted to come."

"I'd really love to, but I'm not sure I can. Could give me directions, and I'll do my best to try?"

The man became uneasy, as if he weren't sure how to respond. I hoped I hadn't said the wrong thing.

"Ah. Well, yes. Sure, I can do that—but only if you promise that you will come."

I had just explained I wasn't sure I could make it. His condition for giving me directions seemed off the mark.

"I'm sorry. Really, I would love to go, but I can't promise I'll be able to."

The man's expression dimmed. That was not what he wanted to hear. I wasn't sure if I'd given him the impression I'd taken his invitation too lightly, or if I'd just made a very wise move and avoided some sort of disastrous predicament. Yet another frustrating catch-22—a sign in and of itself something was awry, although I was too conflicted to realize it at the time.

The passengers began to pile onto the bus, prompting me to turn back around after thanking the man again for the invitation.

The rest of the way to Fez, self-doubt ate away at me. Had I had done the right thing? Or had all the hassling made me overly suspicious? Was it going to be impossible for me to connect with any honest, genuine Moroccans because I would never be able to let my guard down? I was relieved not to have gotten myself into a situation that was uncomfortable or even dangerous, but the possibility I had just passed up a once-in-a-lifetime opportunity filled me with dread. I didn't know what to think.

An hour later, the bus stopped on the outskirts of Fez. I turned around to acknowledge my potential host as he got off. He, however, was nowhere to be found. It was the first and only stop since our conversation, yet the Moroccan had vanished into thin air.

Walking around the medina in Fez, I crossed paths with an Australian I'd seen a few times in Chefchaouen. In his mid-30s like me, his hat looked ideal for adventures in the outback, and he wore the clothes to match. He had a handsome face, with kind eyes and a warm smile, and his body was tall and lanky.

We hadn't spoken in Chefchaouen, but seeing each other again proved an easy icebreaker. In what turned out to be one of several impromptu support groups I'd join during my travels, soon we were sitting at an outdoor café indulging in a honey-flavored shisha and commiserating about the challenges of travel in Morocco.

The Australian, whose name was Peter, had started his trip in Nepal, where the highlight had been catching giardia while rafting in the Himalayas.

"I lost all control of my bowels—it was coming out both ends. They ended up tying me to the back of the raft and dragging me the whole way down the river. It wasn't my proudest moment, but there was nothing else to do."

After confiding that food poisoning had left me vomiting at every rest stop from one side of the Rif mountains to the other, I shifted the conversation to more timely matters.

"Sometimes I just get so frustrated!" I lamented. "I don't want to be mean, but it's so hard to know who to trust. Like the guy who approached me on the bus. He was nice enough, and he even ended up inviting me to his sister's wedding. I didn't know what to do. He didn't seem like a con man, but I just couldn't find it in myself to trust him. So I didn't go to the wedding, and it's been bothering me ever since. I can't stop wondering if I let an amazing opportunity pass me by just because all the harassment has made me so suspicious."

Although Peter had been very talkative until then, he just looked at me with a blank stare. It was almost as if I'd said something to annoy him, though I couldn't imagine what.

After another awkward moment in which he appeared to be

grappling with a difficult decision, two words fell from his mouth.

"You didn't."

"I didn't what?"

"You didn't let an amazing opportunity pass you by."

"Really?"

It seemed strange for him to talk with such confidence about something he ostensibly knew nothing about.

"Why do you say that?"

"I swore to myself I wasn't going to tell anyone this, ever..." he hesitated. "It's so embarrassing."

He paused again, as though reconsidering whether or not to go through with his confession.

Then I got it.

"You met him, too! You met the same guy, didn't you? No way!"

A day earlier, Peter had taken a bus from Chefchaouen to Fez, just I had done that afternoon. At a stop along the way, he, too, had been approached by a friendly, well-dressed Moroccan who struck up a conversation.

"German?" asked the man, no doubt basing his guess on Peter's dishwater blond hair and light blue eyes.

"Australian," Peter responded, for what seemed like the thousandth time.

"Ah! Australian! Then you must be used to this heat! I have a brother who is a doctor in Australia, so I know how hot it gets Down Under!"

"I'm not sure you ever really get used to it. What part of Australia does your brother live in?" Peter began to relax. The guy seemed friendly enough, and it wasn't as if anything bad could happen on a bus.

"Well, where do you live?"

"I'm from Sydney."

"I see. My brother lives in Melbourne."

"Oh really. Have you been?"

"No, unfortunately I've never been able to go, but I hope

to next year. I live in France, and I'm just here for a couple of weeks visiting my family. Are you going to Fez?"

"Uh huh. Is that where you're from?"

"Yes. I was driving there, but my car broke down, so I had to catch this bus instead."

"Your car broke down in the middle of the desert? Sorry to hear that, mate!"

"Yes, it was very bad, but at least the bus came not too long after. You know, since you are going to Fez I invite you to come to my sister's wedding. It is going to be wonderful, and I can tell that you are a nice guy. It would be a great opportunity for you to see a traditional Berber wedding, and you could stay with my family."

"Oh, wow," Peter replied, surprised by the invitation, which seemed so out of the blue. "Thanks a lot, but I really couldn't do that."

"No, no, no! It's no problem! This is Morocco and we love to receive guests and share our culture. We would be honored to have you be there. Of course, if you're don't think it sounds nice or don't want to come..."

"No—it's not that. It sounds great, but...well, when is it?"

Peter was intrigued. He'd just been presented with an unexpected opportunity to experience something few tourists ever get the chance to, and it was very tempting. Yet, while it was true he didn't want to impose, what actually held him back was his reluctance to trust his potential host.

He considered the circumstances in which they had met. They were on a bus, and it was only by chance they were sitting in neighboring rows. If the bus hadn't stopped, they probably wouldn't even be talking at all. The man was in fact dressed nicely enough to be going to a wedding, and he hadn't asked for anything. There really wasn't any reason not to trust him—other than the fact he was Moroccan.

Peter hated himself for thinking that way. Was he now racist? No, after all the challenges he'd faced since arriving in Morocco, that wasn't fair either. He couldn't blame himself for having his guard up. He'd be a fool not to.

"It's tonight. That's why I think it would be very easy for you to come."

The man's enthusiasm had clearly begun to wane, and Peter feared he might have offended him.

"Well, okay," he agreed, overcoming his hesitation. "Yeah. It sounds great—if you're really sure it's no trouble."

The possibility he might miss a wonderful opportunity because he'd become too paranoid to trust anyone had emboldened him, and he'd decided to take the risk.

The man lit back up like a lottery winner, overjoyed by the news. "Wonderful! That's absolutely wonderful! Our stop is the first one in Fez—I'll tell you when it is time."

The passengers began to pile back onto the bus, obliging Peter to face forward when the man seated next to him returned.

After dozing off, Peter opened his eyes to discover the bus had arrived in the outskirts of what appeared to be a large town. Were they in Fez? Turning around to ask, instead of his new friend, Peter was startled to find two older women in traditional dress smiling back at him. Scanning the other rows of passengers, he spied his host all the way in the rear of the bus, chatting with another Moroccan. Feeling Peter's eyes fall upon him, he looked his way, giving him a quick nod and a reassuring smile, without pausing from his conversation.

"That's funny," Peter said to himself. "The whole time I thought he was sitting right behind me."

The bus rambled on for another five or ten minutes before coming to a halt.

"This is it! Hurry, let's go!" The man suddenly at his side, Peter was caught up in an unexpected rush to get off the bus, hurriedly gathering his things as the Moroccan ushered him out of the vehicle as though it were about to burst into flames.

Rather than arriving at a terminal, they had simply pulled over to the side of the road. Only a couple of other passengers got off, both soon gone without a trace. The surrounding area felt more like a forgotten ghost town than the edge of a bustling urban center. Peter couldn't help but feel apprehensive. Did he really want to get off here? At least now he was in Fez. If he did get into some sort of trouble, he wasn't in the middle of nowhere.

It only felt that way.

The Moroccan rushed him over to an empty café.

"How far are we from the center of town?" Peter wondered, in need of a little reassurance.

"Oh, not far. Would you like some mint tea?"

Before Peter could answer, the man called out something to the waiter.

"I have to buy some things for the wedding. It won't take long. Why don't you wait here, and I'll be back shortly."

"Well, okay. But I don't mind..." Peter was about to say he was happy to tag along, but he wasn't given the chance. Not only had his tea arrived, but a distraught expression had overtaken the Moroccan's face.

"Oh no," the man said, as though he had just received horrible news.

"Oh no!" he muttered again, adding something in Arabic.

Already questioning his decision to get off the bus, the drastic change in the man's demeanor made Peter even more uncomfortable.

"It's just...it's just that I had to spend all my money getting the car taken to the mechanic and then buying the bus ticket. I don't have a single dirham left to buy the things I need! I would go into the city for money and come back, but I'm already late and the wedding is going to start and there won't be time...but I can't go with nothing. It would not be right. Besides, I promised my mother I would bring her some things that she needed today. She's counting on me. I can't go this way, it's not possible—not with nothing."

The man was overcome with despair.

"Won't your family understand when you explain what happened?" Peter offered.

His comment fell on deaf ears. The Moroccan was becoming more distressed by the moment, muttering to himself more and more in Arabic and saying less and less in

English.

"My friend," he began, regaining some of his composure, as though he had stumbled upon a way out of his predicament, "we are going to see my family. They will have money, and I am sure they can pay you back right away. I hate to have to ask you this, I really do, but would it be possible for you lend me some money—just until we get to my sister's wedding? I give you my word that you will get your money back as soon as we are there."

Peter felt completely put on the spot.

What the man was saying was entirely plausible. Peter already knew his car had broken down, so it wasn't much of a stretch to imagine he'd been forced to spend more money than planned dealing with the unforeseen crisis. What's more, if it were true and Peter was simply being paranoid, it wasn't fair to the man, especially in his time of need—especially when he had been kind and generous enough to invite him to his sister's wedding.

Assuming they were actually going to a wedding.

Was there really a wedding? It was the first time it had occurred to him to question it. Now that he had, he felt that much more unsettled.

All of his earlier suspicions reappeared out of nowhere, like cobras popping out of their baskets, seductively swaying from side to side as they prepared to strike. Something was not right. He never should have gotten off the bus.

But the bus was long gone.

The man, on the other hand, was sitting right there, anxiously awaiting an answer. Peter didn't have any concrete reasons to discount anything he was saying. Just baseless suspicions. Just because he was in unfamiliar territory. Just because he was afraid to trust anyone. It was hardly enough to call the man a liar to his face.

"How much?"

The words stuck to Peter's tongue like stale baklava. He couldn't believe he had even said them.

The man asked for the equivalent of approximately $35.

"Only if it's not too much. I assure you that you will be paid back as soon as we are at the wedding, which will be in no time at all, really. I hope you don't mind. I feel horrible having to ask this, but I can tell you are a good man. You are very, very kind."

Why did the man need so much? What did he have to buy? $35 wasn't a sum that would leave Peter in financial ruin if it were never returned, but neither was it a trivial amount for a low-budget traveler just out of school.

Despite his monumental misgivings, the pressure was too much. His hands no longer his own, Peter found himself opening his wallet. As he forked over the cash, he had no doubt: he would never see it again.

"Thank you! Thank you so much! You are a good man! I will go to buy the things and be back very soon!"

The man bolted down a side street, leaving Peter alone with his mint tea.

And his regret.

He was dumbfounded, unspeakably disappointed with himself. He couldn't believe that, despite being fully aware of what was happening, he'd gone through with it. How could he be so foolish? He had been right to question the man's motives, and he never should have second-guessed himself. He felt like an idiot.

"I just didn't have the guts to call the guy a thief to his face. I guess it was harder for me to do that than it was to part with the money. I can't tell you how stupid I felt afterwards though. I've been kicking myself ever since."

"Just like I have!" I reminded him, hoping it might come as at least some consolation.

For my part, I couldn't have been more grateful for the synchronous twist of fate that had put a welcome end to my own nagging self-doubt. I had done the right thing after all, the entire experience an important reminder never to underestimate the lengths to which con artists would go to concoct convincing scams. A vital lesson, since I would meet plenty more of them further down the road.

4 WELCOME BACK

The arid landscapes of both Spain and Morocco were in sight for most of our trip across the Strait. Exposed to fierce winds and a merciless sun, it wasn't long before Sophie and I questioned our decision to stand outside. Nevertheless, we were still there two hours later when Tangier appeared in the distance, a subtle sliver of white atop a glittering sea of blue.

Extending across the horizon like two arms opening to receive us, a port gradually took form. Reaching higher and higher the closer we got, a hill covered in small, light-colored buildings with flat roofs rose over it. The dwellings were packed so densely together it was hard to imagine streets running between them. Minarets jutted up into the air, ensuring their mosques weren't lost in the crowd, while a steeple halfway up the hill did the same for a church. No doubt it was a remnant from the days when Europeans and Americans had controlled the city.

Each time I told Sophie a horror story from my previous trip, I made sure to end on a positive note. As we approached the port now, I felt the need to throw out the possibility that our impending arrival would bear no resemblance to my last. Especially since the tourist season was over, it could even prove completely uneventful. When I looked into the water during the crossing and was stunned to find a shark glaring up at me, its eyes, mouth, and teeth all in plain sight, I tried not to take it as a bad omen.

In what turned out to be the biggest shock of my return to Morocco—with one major exception, which wouldn't come until much later—our arrival was in fact painless. There was no mob. No one followed us. We weren't hassled, insulted, or threatened. Even when we got a little off track heading up to the medina, no one swooped in to prey on our confusion.

Perhaps they were all too distracted by Sophie's breasts.

Much to her disdain, Sophie's ample bosom was making even bigger waves than the ones we'd encountered crossing the Strait. Even I noticed it. It was hard not to, since none of the gawkers saw much, if any, need for discretion. Sophie may as well have been wearing a bikini top. The fact that her backpack pulled her shoulders back and made her chest stick out that much further didn't help.

Despite being intelligent, accomplished, and well-traveled, ordinarily Sophie didn't turn a lot of heads. Standing just an inch or two over five feet tall, though she had a great sense of humor that occasionally lit it up, more often than not her face appeared pallid and weary from too many long nights at the office. She rarely dressed in bright colors, and her short, choppy hair unfailingly looked as though it had been cut with a machete. In all our years of friendship, I couldn't recall ever having seen her brush it.

Unsavory ogling aside, we made it to our hotel without incident. It seemed like a great sign, and it left me feeling much more optimistic about the days ahead. Perhaps Morocco had changed.

I was about to find out.

5 RAZOR'S EDGE

Sophie and I spent the day after our arrival exploring Tangier, beginning with the markets in the medina. Wandering through their crowded, chaotic lanes, we saw colorful displays of every kind of fruit and vegetable imaginable. We passed stall after stall of just-slaughtered meat, violent shades of red and the purest of whites hanging from hooks. Entrails were on offer, as were entire animal heads, smiling as though relieved to be rid of their bodies. Conspicuously lacking, on the other hand, were refrigerated display cases, everything out in the open, exposed to the heat and humidity—and flies, persistent swarms of which vied for first dibs on the freshest cuts.

In an area the size of a small warehouse we perused all sorts of seafood caught earlier in the day. A musty saltwater smell filled the air, and the floor, too, was slick with the sea. Even Sophie, whose father was a fisherman, was unable to identify much of what was on display. Elsewhere we saw vendors selling dates or olives or dried fruits and nuts, each offering impressive varieties of their specialties. There were tempting selections of sweets, and a broad array of spices arranged in picture-perfect, cone-shaped piles, their colors so striking they could have easily been taken for dyes.

Heading back outside, we wound our way towards the

kasbah, or citadel, strategically situated at the highest point in the medina. Although home to a museum I was looking forward to visiting again, there was an even more important reason the kasbah was not to be missed.

As we entered one side of a large square enclosed by the fortress walls, on the other we saw an arched stone gate. Opening onto nothing but clear blue sky, it looked like an image taken from a surrealist's dream, one of Magritte's paintings come to life.

Crossing the square and passing through the gate, we were greeted by violent gusts of wind and an extraordinary view of the Strait of Gibraltar, where the Atlantic Ocean and the Mediterranean Sea converge. From our privileged vantage point high above it all, we saw rugged cliffs plummeting into tumultuous blue waters, occasional white specks betraying vessels far below. Spain was in plain view, once again surprising us with how close the two countries—the two continents—were to one another. It was spectacular, and we weren't the only ones to think so. The ancient Greeks referred to the area as the Pillars of Hercules, and they considered it the end of the known world.

Although I, too, was appreciating the awe-inspiring view, what Sophie had no way of knowing was that I was also having flashbacks. When I noticed a little boy somewhere around the age of ten approaching, I decided it was time to go—just to be safe. I didn't tell Sophie why. She looked at me perplexed, but followed without protest.

After a day and a half in Tangier, my curiosity had been satisfied. I had made my triumphant return, and it had gone well—better than expected, in fact. No need to press my luck by traveling deeper into the country. Except I had already broached the subject with Sophie. Tangier was an interesting introduction but, for someone who had never been to Morocco, at the very least a visit to Fez or Marrakech was a must. When I asked her about it again, she didn't miss a beat.

We were going to Fez.

As we started to ponder logistics, an incident a short distance away brought our conversation to a halt.

A dirty, disheveled old man, his exact age indiscernible beneath wild grey locks and a full, unkempt beard, appeared in the small square where we were having tea. Initially, we took little notice of him. That all changed when without warning he ripped off his coat—under which he had no shirt—and began screaming in Arabic. He then produced what was either a knife or a razor, extended his left arm, and began slicing himself in brisk, determined strokes. Blood began to flow and the people around him recoiled, aghast at the startling turn of events.

Looking more closely, I noticed the man already had streaks of blood all over his body, some brighter than others. Even his head was covered in them, as though he'd been attacked by a bird of prey.

He continued slicing himself, each time as shocking to behold as the last. More and more blood poured down his arm, and he kept yelling things Sophie and I couldn't understand.

A loud ruckus ensued, men rushing at the old man from all sides. One bravely wrested away the sharp object, while others restrained him. Even as he was escorted from the square, he carried on with his ranting and raving.

What was going on in his head? Was he on drugs? Was he mentally ill? And why the horrific slashing? Could whatever emotional pain he might be feeling possibly be worse than the physical pain to which he was publicly subjecting himself? Or was he like two of my high school friends, who had discreetly cut incision after incision into their own skin in the hopes of feeling anything at all?

Whatever the explanation, the spectacle was profoundly disturbing. Even after it was over, I couldn't shake the bizarre, defiant expression on the old man's face. It was as if he were seeing some brutal truth none of the rest of us dared acknowledge.

Ten minutes later he was back.

Sophie and I stopped our conversation, wondering what to expect this time. The man, however, was perfectly calm. The storm seemed to have passed. He probably was mentally ill, after all, and what we had witnessed before was likely some sort of fit.

But then, again without warning, he launched into another diatribe, directing his vitriol at a café worker who had assisted in his apprehension shortly before.

The worker approached the old man. It appeared they might even know each other, that it might not be the first time the scenario had played out.

Whether or not the old man was crazy, he wasn't stupid. As the café worker got closer, the old man turned to onlookers and passers-by, beseeching them to take his side—to believe whatever story he was trying to sell them.

Much to our astonishment, it worked.

After two women began gesturing for the café worker to back off, others in the fast-growing crowd jumped on the bandwagon. A man stepped forward to prevent the café worker from laying a hand on the old man. A few people began jeering, while others argued amongst themselves or shook their heads in disgrace.

Sophie and I were astounded by the ease with which the conniving old man had manipulated an entire crowd, almost effortlessly turning them against the café worker. Had they even stopped to question what they were being told? Was there nothing about the old man's appearance or behavior that gave them pause for thought?

It was a disturbing lesson in mob psychology.

6 GETTING STONED

The next morning Sophie and I checked out of our hotel and walked to the train station, located on the outskirts of town beyond a barren wasteland of vacant, overgrown lots. Looking out the window as we headed south, we saw impoverished villages separated from the tracks by vast fields of garbage. Although we'd witnessed many other reminders of the harsh economic realities facing the country, it didn't make these any less heartbreaking.

We were even more shocked when something struck the side of our train.

I scanned the landscape, settling on a group of little boys scarcely able to contain their glee, laughing uncontrollably as they egged each other on. From what I could tell, they were competing to see who could pelt the train with the most rocks before it left behind their village. Assuming no windows were shattered, it was a relatively harmless game—other than the jolt it gave unsuspecting passengers. It was also one of which we'd repeatedly be a part over the course of our trip.

I couldn't help but think of the experience I'd failed to share with Sophie the day before, since it, too, involved boys throwing stones. I decided now was a good time to tell her.

On my first visit to the lookout in Tangier, I had been much more relaxed. I had recovered from my harrowing arrival the night before and, apparently having passed some sort of unspoken rite of passage, the next day I'd been left alone. No one even seemed to care I was there. It was a bizarre shift from one extreme to the other, but I wasn't complaining.

Sitting down on a low concrete wall to take in the incredible view, it wasn't long before I was surrounded by a group of small boys. None of them could have been more than ten years old. Despite being as rough around the edges as their dirty, ragged clothes, they were adorable. As they came closer, I couldn't help but smile at the way they looked up at me with their big dark eyes and bright, mischievous smiles.

One of the boys began speaking to me in Spanish.

"Hola."

"Hola," I replied

"¿Cómo está Ud.?" he asked, as if reading from a phrasebook.

"Bien, ¿y Ud.?" I replied, addressing him in the same formal case he had respectfully used with me, even though an adult wouldn't ordinarily use it with a child.

"Bien. ¿Español?" he inquired.

"Bueno, más o menos." I didn't mind chatting, but I was sick of being asked my nationality.

One of the other boys said something in Arabic. An awkward pause followed during which the first boy seemed to have run out of things to say. More likely he was debating whether or not to cut to the chase. I readied myself for the inevitable.

"¿Un dirham, por favor?" he asked coyly, extending his hand so I could fill it with change.

I didn't say anything. Instead, I smiled to acknowledge the game had begun and shook my head "no".

"¡Un dirham! ¡Un dirham señor!" other voices chimed in, countless hands shooting into the air.

I felt like a mother bird returning empty-handed to a volatile brood. There were seven or eight boys in the group, all deviously staring up at me, almost assuredly having been through this a thousand times before. I wasn't going to give them anything. Our nascent friendship would be over before it began.

"No," I replied calmly but resolutely.

They had expected as much. Undeterred, they repeated their demands.

"*¡Un dirham! ¡Un dirham!*" they insisted, their welcoming smiles wiped from their faces, replaced by pursed lips and furrowed brows. An occasional laugh slipped out, as a couple of boys struggled to stay in character.

"Nooooooo," I droned, deliberately being silly in the hopes of calling their bluff. I also hoped that if I could convince them of my resolve, they'd drop it. The same tactic having proven utterly useless a day earlier, I'm not sure why I thought that. On the other hand, these were just innocent children. Surely they weren't capable of the same belligerence as the men from the day before.

My tactic worked. Unable to keep up their ruse, the boys broke into a spontaneous chorus of giggles. My comical response had caught them off guard, and they seemed delighted by it.

I figured laughter was a good sign. Now that they knew I wasn't going to give them anything, the game was over. We were all on the same page, and we could relax. No hard feelings.

"He wants to fuck you," the boy from before uttered out of nowhere, motioning to one of his friends. I was blindsided. The shock must have shown on my face, because the whole group broke into even bigger laughter than before.

I was suddenly very, very uncomfortable.

"You shouldn't talk like that," I admonished, as if the boys were going to pay any mind to a scolding from me, a random tourist who couldn't spare a dirham. Besides, they knew exactly what they were doing. They'd caught me off guard and gotten the exact response they wanted.

"He has a big ass," added the boy, provoking more raucous laughter, this time louder still. His friends were besides themselves—even the boy who was the butt of the joke.

It was time to leave. While being wrongfully jailed for pedophilia in Morocco would have made an amazing story, it wasn't worth it. I imagined defending myself to the judge, "But your honor, I swear, the ten-year-old boy was coming on to me!"

What I couldn't imagine was having heard the word "fuck" at their age, never mind knowing it in another language. Even if I had heard it, I wouldn't have known what it meant, nor would it have ever occurred to me to even jokingly (I really hoped they were joking and believed they were) employ it as a proposition. How had these innocent little boys, their tiny bodies not even approaching pubescence, learned such things? I tried to convince myself they didn't know what they were saying. My gut said otherwise.

Hopping off the wall, I stole one last look at the Strait before taking leave of the gang, praying they wouldn't follow me.

The boys continued to laugh and jeer behind my back, now in Arabic since they no longer needed to make themselves understood by me, the greedy stranger. At least they weren't pursuing me.

It was then that a stone pelted my shoulder blade.

"Oh god," I said to myself, trying to dismiss what I prayed was a brazen but isolated act. One of the boys was probably just trying to prove himself to the others. But what if they followed his example? My back was turned. Unless I threw myself over the trash-strewn cliff, I had nowhere to go until I got to the gate. I was a very easy target.

The boys thought so, too.

The second rock to make contact hit my lower back. Fortunately, it didn't hurt as much as the first. Another whizzed past my left ear, just barely missing. My reflexes belatedly kicking in, I couldn't help but flinch. The children cheered, relishing having reduced me to their plaything.

Fifteen to twenty feet remained between me and the gate. Torn between my pride, which refused to give the children the thrill of seeing me make a run for it, and my survival instincts, which demanded I get the hell out of there before being stoned to death, I opted for somewhere in between.

Taking a cue from those perky athletes who somehow manage to walk really, really fast without breaking into an actual jog, I switched into high gear, redefining the limits of what can technically be considered walking. If instead of outside the walls of an ancient kasbah, I'd been making circles inside a mall, there wouldn't have been a single walker from Macy's to Footlocker who wouldn't have been awestruck.

It occurred to me that if I turned around and made a scene or even threw a couple of stones at the kids, they were almost sure to disperse. Running in all directions, they'd find themselves dispossessed of the safety and courage of the mob. But if an adult happened to observe the scene at the wrong time, how would I explain throwing rocks at a group of little boys? Better to play it cool and let them have the sort of fun with me they might have with a stray dog.

Rocks still flying, I made it through the gate mostly unscathed. A barrier between worlds, on the other side it was business as usual. A couple of traditionally dressed Moroccan men walked through the square. Some European tourists approached the entrance to the museum. No one gave me a second look. Neither did they notice when I slipped out of the square. My heart still beating fast, I headed back to the hotel to lick my wounds.

7 OVERTURE, CURTAIN LIGHTS

After an obligatory change of trains, Sophie and I found ourselves sharing a compartment for eight with four other passengers. What appeared to be a grandfather, father, and son trio sat next to the window. An older woman in bright blue traditional garb sat in one of the seats next to the door, her head covered though she didn't wear a veil.

Sophie sat across from me reading a newspaper, while I was lost in a book. When the time came to flip a page, I glanced at the mirror over Sophie's head, noticing a young man looking furtively into our compartment. He could have been debating whether or not to take the empty seats. Given the calculating look on his face and the fact he and his friend had already passed by multiple times, I suspected what actually interested him was Sophie and I. I became uneasy, wondering if it was time to brace myself for another round.

It was.

The door slid open, as though breaking a hermetic seal protecting us from infection from the outside world. Rather than the guy who'd been watching us, I was surprised to discover his friend. In his late 30s or early 40s, everything about him suggested he was the furthest thing imaginable from a threat. Clean-cut with a warm, gentle demeanor, he smiled as he squeezed into the compartment, looking everyone in the eyes and apologizing whenever his short but solid body brushed against ours. It made things easier that he didn't carry any bags. When Sophie moved over a seat to make room, he and I found ourselves face-to-face. He smiled again and said hello.

Before he had the chance to say more, his cohort reappeared, animated, wise-cracking, and ready to become the best of friends with anyone he came across. In this case, that just so happened to be Sophie and I. He took the seat next to me and made some predictable small talk—where were we from, he couldn't help but ask—before mysteriously disappearing again.

His much more reserved yet just as amicable friend picked up where he left off. It felt like an introductory meeting for an arranged marriage. Sophie and I had been left alone with the reserved one to get to know him better, in the hopes we'd all hit it off. It was only a matter of time before the extrovert reappeared to see how things were going, the doting mother excited about her daughter's prospects with a prospective suitor.

Our new best friend explained that he lived and worked in Germany. Since his family lived in Fez, he returned periodically to visit—that is, when he didn't travel instead to any of the numerous international destinations he also liked to go on holiday. His current trip home was to last three weeks, including drive time from Germany to Spain and stops at multiple destinations in Morocco.

It all sounded eerily familiar. It sounded almost identical, in fact, to a conversation I had once had on a bus from Chefchaouen. Of course, just like on that bus ride, none of what the Moroccan was saying was remotely implausible. Attempting not to jump to any conclusions, I did my best to withhold judgment while still keeping my guard up.

It's hard to say how much time elapsed before the extrovert returned. When he did, he made sure no one failed to notice. Throwing open the door with all the subtlety of a novice

Broadway performer, he took to the stage. Even the lights seemed to dim, all eyes in the compartment turned expectantly towards him. There was no doubt: we were about to be treated to quite a show.

Several years younger than his friend, the extrovert allegedly worked as some sort of student exchange coordinator. Tall, dark, and almost as handsome as he thought he was, if he'd been delivering punches instead of one-liners, Sophie and I would have been knocked unconscious in record time. This was a young man with star quality—all you had to do was ask, and he was sure to tell you so himself.

The more he turned up the charm, the less I trusted him. While he tried to endear himself with endless, unconvincing banter, I kept a hypervigilant eye on our belongings. I made sure I knew where our bags were. I confirmed the pants pocket with my wallet and passport was zipped. I maintained an unfaltering eye on Sophie and her pockets, too.

It wasn't long before his antics got to be too much. The old man next to the window began shooting me knowing looks that seemed intended to confirm my suspicions, and I was growing more and more impatient. Something had to give. It finally did.

"So, where are you guys staying in Fez?"

About time. Now we were getting somewhere. I knew this part of the script. Whereas ordinarily it would have annoyed me, this time the familiar line came as a relief. I just wanted to play out the little drama, so we could get it over and done with.

I made some sort of vague, noncommittal reply.

It turned out the extrovert just happened to know a great hotel. The only problem was that since he'd never recommended it to anyone, he blanked on the name. Just our luck! Fortunately, his memory lapse proved fleeting, and moments later he was able to recall not only the hotel's name but its location. I thanked him politely, vowing to avoid it at all costs.

"So," he continued, directing his question at Sophie, "what are you going to buy in Fez?"

She hesitated, saying she wasn't sure or didn't know or something along those lines.

Not having gotten the response he'd hoped for, he turned to me, his good 'ole buddy.

"What about you? What are you going to buy?"

"Nothing."

"Nothing?" It was as though the train had slammed to a halt. The very notion someone could even consider going to Fez without buying something was so heretical, it took him a moment to regroup. "Don't you want to support the local artisans?"

"I'm already spending lots of money on hotels and food and other things. Don't worry about me not doing my part," I reassured him.

"But you have to buy something!" he insisted, as though my brutal asceticism genuinely pained him.

"Morocco has lots of beautiful things I would honestly love to buy," I explained. "And hopefully one day I will, when I have lots of money. On this trip, though, we're not here very long, so we just want to spend some time walking around."

"That's right," chimed in the woman next to the door, catching us both off guard. The extrovert and I had been speaking French. Until then, in no way had she let on that she'd been following along. "He doesn't have to buy anything if he doesn't want to. It's enough that he's come at all, and we should receive him with open arms."

A beautiful woman with a dark complexion, full lips, and reflective brown eyes, she expressed herself with the poise and dignity of someone who has lived a righteous life. I appreciated her intervention.

Little could I have known, she was only getting started.

Directing her attention exclusively to the extrovert, she switched to Arabic and went off on him. Her severe, accusatory tone and emphatic gestures, coupled with his startled expression, left no doubt: she was scolding him, presumably for badgering us. Not for a moment did she lose her composure, but she spoke with such intensity that the men next to the window stopped their conversation, too, hanging onto her every word. Most telling of all, even the extrovert shut up for the duration.

When the tirade was over, he preferred not to share the specifics. Instead, proving he was capable of brevity when it suited him, he limited his summary to, "She doesn't think I'm a good Muslim."

He then laughed it off. All in good fun.

"You know, tonight after we get to Fez, we should meet for coffee."

I was astonished. Even after being publicly shamed, the extrovert refused to let up. On the bright side, he'd just given me the last red flag I needed. This was, as I had suspected from the start, the typical con.

They began by showing us how much we had in common, since one lived in Europe and the other worked with foreigners. They then built up a rapport and—so they thought—the all important trust. Once that was established, they transitioned to the familiar lines of questioning: Where were we staying? What were we going to buy? Why didn't we meet up later?

Not missing a beat—knowing we'd reached a critical juncture—I jumped in before Sophie had a chance to respond, politely yet firmly insisting, "Thank you very much, but we can't. We don't have much time, and we just kind of want to do our own thing."

"Oh, come on!" protested the extrovert, shifting his focus from me to Sophie, hoping to have better luck. "You know these Americans," he laughed, "they can't trust anybody."

Now he had gone too far.

It wasn't what he had said. Coming from him, a pathetic affront to any feelings of patriotism I might have meant nothing. What pushed me over the edge was the tactic itself. Like so many before him, the extrovert thought that by shocking us with statements we were supposed to feel obliged to contradict, he could manipulate us into doing his bidding. It was as juvenile as transparent, and I was tired of it. The irony, of course, was that he was right: I didn't trust anyone. No one, that is, in Morocco who approached me for no reason. But it wasn't about paranoia or racism or religion. It was about lessons learned from past experience.

"How about coffee tomorrow morning?" he ventured again.

"No." I said without elaborating. I wanted him gone. Now.

He turned back to Sophie, and I withdrew from the conversation, though still paying close attention. At some point he must have realized I was the one he'd have to convince, because he suddenly looked at me and asked one more time, "So, come on. You're really not going to meet us for coffee?"

It was incredible. Like so many before him, he was relentless. His refusal to take "no" for an answer was the clearest sign yet that something was up.

As I will demonstrate later, even when provoked I'm not one to resort to violence. Having been hassled, lied to, and insulted yet again in a country I was beginning to regret having given a second chance, however, the thought of doing physical harm to the extrovert was becoming more tempting each time he opened his mouth.

I guess it showed.

His friend, who hadn't said anything for quite a while, jumped into the conversation—in Arabic, for the first time since joining us. Then, taking over from his friend, who miraculously had been silenced for a second time, he turned to me and said, "I think you're very smart."

"You think so?" I retorted, assuming he was being sarcastic.

"Yeah," he calmly replied, without a hint of malice.

It was a strange moment. I had the impression of sitting on the other side of a chessboard from an opponent who, rather than feeling ill-will upon conceding defeat, has that much more respect for their adversary.

If any doubt remained the duo were con artists, it all went up in smoke when without warning they got up to leave. Although it was all friendly and good-natured, with hands shaken and well wishes exchanged, there was one glaring issue:

we weren't anywhere near a stop.

If we were all headed to the same destination and so thoroughly enjoying each other's company, why were they leaving? And where were they going?

I didn't bother to ask, keeping my mouth shut and counting my blessings as I closed the door behind them.

8 A TURKISH BATH IN MOROCCO

Sophie and I spent a fun day-and-a-half in Fez. We wandered aimlessly through the colorful, chaotic labyrinth of alleys making up the medina, the air heavy with dust and spices, charged with a relentless tension, everything in motion. We went into shops full of ceramics, carpets, and woodwork, all handmade by local artisans. We perused antiques once treasured by medina families or salvaged from desert kasbahs. We looked at mirrors framed with decorative tin or inlaid wood, and we tried on babouches that called to mind shoes a genie would wear.

When we'd practically worn our own shoes thin, we stopped at a café. As we sipped mint tea made from whole, fresh leaves, we watched merchants, residents, and tourists alike make their ways up and down the lane. Later, having resumed our wanderings, we had to jump to the side when a horse came storming out of nowhere, cart in tow. Sophie and I laughed nervously in its wake. Surprised such a large animal could even fit into such a tight space, we were glad not to have been trampled.

When a boy along the way presented us with an unexpected opportunity, we took him up on it. Not much older than the youngsters who had made such a lasting impression in Tangier, he wasn't nearly as scruffy. Neither was he as insistent, sparing us the hard sell. After settling on a reasonable price, he took us to a rooftop overlooking an unlikely and surprisingly large open space, still within the tightly packed confines of the medina. Honeycombed with row after row of earthen vats, each was full of a red, tan, or grey liquid. Some had people standing in them.

We had come to the leather tanneries, one of Fez's most renowned sites. Looking up at us with eager brown eyes, the boy explained in broken English that the tanning and dyeing processes were undertaken in essentially the same fashion they had been for thousands of years. It smelled like something had been festering down there just as long. When the boy added that the ingredients used included fish oil, cow urine, pigeon excrement, and animal brains, we understood why.

Walking past a Turkish bath, or hammam, Sophie joked that after visiting the tanneries, we should probably go inside for a scrubdown.

"Feel free," I cringed.

"What? You don't like hammams?" she asked.

"I had a bad experience in one."

Since it, too, had taken place in Morocco, I proceeded to tell her the story.

During the entire year I lived in Istanbul, I never made it to a hammam. Given that I'm ordinarily keen on taking full advantage of the cultural experiences that are unique to—or, especially in this case, even emblematic of—the places I visit, I'd never been able to forgive myself for the oversight.

Just like the old Turkish toilets, those glorified holes in the ground over which countless legions of squatters have played a bizarre sort of scatological target practice, Turkish baths have a long history all their own. Over time they became fixtures not only in their homeland but far beyond its borders, particularly throughout the Arab world.

Consequently, it came as little surprise when, at an otherwise relatively uninspired stop in my travels, I discovered a hammam not far from my hotel. I didn't give it a second thought. The time had come to right a horrible wrong, one that had weighed on my conscience for far, far too long.

I was going to a Turkish bath in Morocco.

I asked the two women at the hotel front desk for the lowdown. I already knew that whereas in Turkey a towel wrapped around the waist was customary, in Morocco men were required to wear bathing suits. I wondered what else I needed to know.

Both women seemed delighted I had not only shown an interest in but was actually about to partake of one of their most hallowed traditions. Taking me under their wings as if temporarily adopting a son, they briefed me on the *dos* and *don'ts*. They also provided me with flip flops and a colorful plastic pail. Feeling like a child headed for a day at the beach, rather than a grown man seeking a deeper connection to a people and place though an ancient ritual, I set off to make peace with my past and expand my cultural horizons.

Easily finding my way to the hammam, I opened the door and stepped inside. A subdued peace and quiet of the sort usually reserved for places of worship reigned over a small lobby, a dimly lit, self-contained world somehow impervious to the blinding midday sun and the cacophony of the city outside.

A staircase climbed upwards to my left, coming to an abrupt halt at a closed door. Benches lined the wall opposite me as well as the one to my right, the reception area also serving as changing room, oddly enough. Under each bench were small cubby holes with doors, while overhead were narrow, cloudy windows more effective at holding the daylight at bay than allowing it inside.

Before beginning the tragic descent into its present state of neglect, the building had seen much better days, signs of its faded glory discernible everywhere I looked. The ceiling that had once soared majestically overhead had been begging for a new coat of paint for years, blemished by peeling patches so deep they exposed bone-white plaster. The carpets were threadbare, their worn fibers like veins stripped of their flesh, and the flight of the once elegant stairway had been grounded, cluttered by haphazard piles of boxes and all sorts of forgotten junk.

On the other side of the room, an old man sat behind a simple desk. He saw me enter, but neither said a word nor moved a muscle. I couldn't help but wonder if he hadn't been there as long as the hammam itself, having become an inseparable part of it, a lover who'd be lost without it. I walked over and inquired how much it would cost to use the baths.

"Would you like a massage?" he asked.

I hadn't expected the question, but I didn't have to think twice about the answer. I'd been traveling for almost a week, burdened by a large backpack and sitting on cramped buses for hours at a time, my back a contorted mass of knots. A massage was exactly what my sore and aching body needed.

I paid the man and found a place on one of the benches. Taking off my clothes, I put on my bathing suit, a little self-conscious doing so in plain sight of the stoic set of eyes observing me such a short distance away. It wasn't until I went to put my belongings in a cubby hole that I noticed there weren't any locks on the doors. The cubbies were little more than cupboards, as opposed to full-fledged lockers. I hesitated, once again turning to the man, who had anticipated my question and gestured dismissively. He was sitting right there, and no one else was around. Besides, I had left my passport and other valuables at the hotel. I didn't have anything to worry about.

Once I was ready, the man ushered me through a door to his right, into a room that might have been unremarkable, had it not contrasted so dramatically with the reception area. It was as if I'd unknowingly made the descent to a lower level of the edifice, a tenebrous netherworld where the walls, floor, and ceiling were all made of the same grey stone. A heavy vapor hung on the air and light was scarce, as though unwelcome there.

I was now alone, uneasy like someone arriving at a haunted house in the middle of nowhere only to find the door close behind them. In this case, however, I was standing in the darkness wearing a bathing suit and flip flops and holding a silly plastic pail I could have been using to build sand castles. Everything seemed a little off.

It wasn't long before an enormous older man emerged out of nowhere. He was, to be sure, an astonishing sight, a fleshy giant with the palest of skin, the thinnest of hair, and the dimmest and dullest of expressions. Everything about him suggested that if he had ever seen the light of day, he had no recollection of it.

Just like me, he carried a bucket, which he dipped into a large basin of steaming water on the other side of the room. Unlike me, he wore an obscenely small, dingy pair of underwear that clung precariously to his sweaty buttocks and groin. Saturated to lurid transparency, it came nowhere close to containing the fleshy undulations of his enormous body. In spite of myself, I stared like a voyeuristic witness to a car wreck, snapped out of my stupor only when he turned and looked my way, our eyes locking.

Diverting my gaze, I wondered where my masseur was. Maybe I was being impatient, but it seemed he was taking an unreasonably long time to come find me. He was probably just finishing up with another customer, I told myself, trying to relax. For all I knew, he was still preparing the room, putting clean sheets on the massage table or making sure he had everything else in order before our session.

Often we discover that what we're looking for is right under our noses.

Although the corpulent behemoth now lumbering towards me wouldn't have come even close to fitting under my nose—which scarcely reached beyond his hairy navel—it turned out that he was, nonetheless, exactly what I had been looking for.

"Massage?" he asked, with what seemed like a mischievous grin. I wondered why he suddenly looked so happy, overwhelmed by the uneasy feeling I was about to become the butt of a very bad joke.

"Ah, yes..." I hesitated, my eyes darting in all directions in the hopes of finding a quick way out. I didn't have the guts to tell him that putting myself at the mercy of a nearly naked ogre three times my size made me a little uncomfortable. Instead, though kicking and screaming inside, outside I offered no resistance, obediently following my captor deeper into the darkness.

While it didn't even come close to the descriptions I had heard of beautiful old marble-covered Turkish hammams, the main chamber wasn't completely devoid of charm. The walls and floor were identical to those in the previous room and, as such, relatively plain; but, the ceiling took the form of an elegant dome perforated by tiny circular windows. Through each of their translucent panes, a precise beam pierced the steamy obscurity, affording the naked eye just enough light to get a sense of the surroundings.

The man gestured for me to sit down on a stone bench and rinse myself with the hot water from the basin. I did so, after which he went to get more. Looking around, I noticed there were only two other men in the hammam, engaged in hushed conversation on the far side of the room. I would have preferred there be a few more people, but at least I was no longer alone.

When the man returned with the water, he seemed to be gesturing for me to get onto the floor. I knew that couldn't be right, but I had no way of asking him to clarify, since my attempts—first in French, then in Spanish, and finally in English—were all met with silence.

Not interested in dilly dallying, the masseur took me by the hand, raising it so I'd stand up. Once I had, he again pointed to the floor, more commandingly this time.

Not only could it be right, but it was.

He wanted me on my knees.

Despite my hesitance, I reluctantly obeyed, reminding myself he was the one who knew how this was all supposed to work, not I. I just had to go with it. Or, to be more precise, I just had to kneel before him, not actually going anywhere at all.

The giant wasted no time dousing my upper body yet again,

only to then unleash a full-on assault with a soapy wet rag. For the first time since entering the hammam, I began to relax. The water was warm and it felt good, as did having someone attentively scrub my body. The deep cleaning went well beyond what I could do on my own, removing layers of all sorts of grime I hadn't even realized was there. I felt something akin to when sitting in a barber's chair, the soothing touch on my scalp always lulling me into a state of utter relaxation, if not gentle slumber.

No sooner had he finished scouring my upper body and arms, than I had the surreal impression the man was making another, even more bizarre request. Rather than merely kneel on the floor, he seemed to be asking me to lie down on it.

I'm not even remotely a germophobe. Unless you're about to perform surgery, I think hand sanitizer is ridiculous, yet another product cleverly designed and ingeniously marketed to keep consumers in a constant state of paranoia. I'll drink from friends' cups, I never bother to put antiseptic on cuts, and I am an unapologetic, lifelong adherent to the three-second rule, rarely having any issues picking up food that's fallen to the floor and putting it into my mouth without the slightest hesitation.

But this wasn't just any floor.

This was a grimy, slimy floor. The same floor on which my maternal hotel guardians had insisted I wear flip flops, an absolute hygienic necessity, protection against an untold number of unimaginable health hazards lying on the damp stone like predators in wait. A floor rising up from which I was almost certain I could hear the mating calls and battle cries of countless unknown strains of bacteria, fungi that were sure to colonize each and every crevice of my body, and viruses that science had yet to develop any means of combating. All of them were glaring up at me like lions pacing about their den, greedily anticipating how they would ravage their next meal when it fell from the sky.

Kowtowing to be at the right level for the masseur to do his job was one thing; pressing my entire body against the mysterious muck on the floor was another altogether.

It didn't matter.

Before I could protest—something I probably wouldn't have done anyway, for reasons I've already explained—the giant had taken me by the shoulders and pushed me towards the floor. By no means was he violent, but neither did he leave any doubt as to what I was supposed to do.

Lying on my back, my body was soon riddled with anxiety like the ceiling was its tiny holes. I could no longer see the masseur, so I had no idea what he was doing—or going to do—and I couldn't stop thinking about the fact I was lying in filth. When my own dead skin, clumps of hair, and unseen microbes had tumbled to the floor, no one had run out from behind a curtain to mop it all up. Who else's dirt, germs, and bodily fluids had welcomed mine as they joined them in a debaucherous orgy? On second thought, never mind. I didn't want to know. After all, it was now all over my back, which, whether merely due to the power of suggestion or because of infectious outbreaks now underway, had begun to itch.

It was then that the giant reappeared, coming between me and the constellation of lights overhead like the moon eclipsing not only the sun but all the stars. Despite the stifling heat, his dark shadow gave me a foreboding chill. For the first time it occurred to me that if he decided to harm me in any way, there wasn't a thing I could do about it—something I struggled with even more as he proceeded to climb all over my body.

Besides having all three-hundred-plus of his fleshy pounds ready to crush me at any moment, should he slip on the wet stone or his arms buckle under his own weight, what was to come involved not only scalding water, but a new rag that may as well have been made of steel wool.

News the next phase was underway shot from one end of my nervous system to the other like a summer wildfire backed by strong winds. Between the blistering temperature of the water and the stinging fibers of the rag, I wasn't sure what hurt more. While I gave it some thought, the giant made his way up my body, beginning with my legs, deferentially bypassing the family jewels, and proceeding up my torso. Once he got to my shoulders, he extended each of my arms as if he were also about to crucify me. Truth be told, it probably would have felt better than what followed.

As though letting out a lifetime of anger to which he'd never been able to give voice, the giant took it up a notch. His massive gut mere inches from my face, he scrubbed my helpless body with a relentless fury. I closed my eyes and shut my mouth as a salty shower of sweat rained down on me, holding my breath. It was agonizing, and I wasn't sure it was ever going to end.

Just as I was about to reach my breaking point, it finally did.

Or so I thought.

While I was still writhing in pain, breathless like a fish flopping around on the bow of a boat, my so-called masseur jumped into a bizarre practice that would have been completely foreign to any massage therapist I've ever known. To a pastry chef, on the other hand, the technique would have been all too familiar.

Like dough that needed to be molded into a perfect pie crust, he began pinching both sides of my torso from top to bottom.

Hard.

It was excruciating—the steel wool paling in comparison. I couldn't help but wonder if there'd be any skin left on my body when the sadistic ritual was finally over.

As I was about to let out a desperate cry that would require no translation, the giant finished putting the final touches on what was essentially the icing on the cake. Successfully making the Herculean effort to stand back up, he then retreated to someplace deep in the hammam's secret underworld, leaving me flinching on the floor like a bug that's been smashed but isn't quite dead. Staring up at the pretty beams of light, I wondered why they were spinning.

I have no idea how long I lay there. I was stunned, struggling with exactly what part of the ordeal could have possibly been considered the "massage". When it finally came time to peel myself from the floor, I felt like an egg stuck to a dirty frying pan—I practically needed someone to scrape me off it. Given that my entire body felt so raw, I also couldn't help but wonder if the giant hadn't drawn blood, which almost seemed to have been his goal.

Once I succeeded in propping myself upright, I sat in the steam for a short while longer, my senses slowly returning to me. Repeatedly reliving the absurd experience in an attempt to make sense of it, I eventually conceded there was no point and decided to head back to the hotel.

No sooner did I get to my room, than I stood in the mirror and took off my shirt.

I hadn't been imagining things.

In the reflection of my torso I beheld four butchered patches of flesh where blood had seeped to the surface. Some of it had already scabbed, while other areas were still speckled with bright red drops of freshly oxygenated blood.

The giant had indeed been so rough he had made me bleed. If lying on the floor of the hammam was potentially risky, what could be the ramifications of doing so with open wounds? I prayed the water had been hot enough to kill any infectious agents and hoped for the best, hand sanitizer no longer seeming like such a bad idea after all.

9 A BUS RIDE IN FEZ

The only noteworthy dark spot on an otherwise bright day in Fez was something that happened near the end of it, on the city bus to our hotel.

Where Sophie and I were in back, it was standing room only. Given the challenges of keeping an eye on things with so many people at such close range, I was a little uneasy. More so than myself, however, I was worried about Sophie. She had purchased a carpet and a few other items in the medina, making her not only more of a target, but less able to protect herself from unseen, wandering hands.

Yet again it turned out I wasn't being paranoid.

I was, however, mistaken about the target.

Tight quarters not withstanding, I kept feeling as though the guy to my left were moving in unnecessarily close. A good-looking fellow in his 30s, his otherwise respectable choices of dark slacks and a white button-down were both long overdue for a laundering. His black hair tumbled to his jawline when not pushed back, and it was slick with the same sweat that gave his face an oily sheen. Was he coming onto me? Was he testing to see if I was paying attention? Whatever the case, it seemed strange. Since I couldn't move because another young man was on my right, I stayed put, paying even closer attention to my surroundings.

It was then that, in my peripheral vision, I could have sworn I saw two fingers reaching for my pocket.

I turned to look.

Nothing.

Still, something felt weird. My gut told me I wasn't imagining things.

As I kept a close eye on Sophie, who was now talking with a friendly Moroccan gentleman, again I had the distinct impression something was happening to my left.

This time I was more subtle. Rather than quickly turning to the side, I kept my head positioned as though I were still looking straight ahead. At the same time, however, I discretely peered out of the corner of my eye to see what, if anything, was going on.

It was.

Two outstretched fingers were reaching for my pocket.

I had caught him in the act.

All the same, I didn't say anything. I was too intrigued, a voyeur to my own violation. No doubt my reaction would have been much different if I hadn't known for certain the pockets within the thief's reach contained nothing of value. Since they didn't, I found the experience fascinating.

The fingers he used surprised me. Rather than his index finger and thumb, he had developed to such a degree the dexterity of his pinky and its neighbor that he could perform his criminal feats with them alone. It was impressive, casting my own lifelong struggles with chop sticks in an even more depressing light.

The other tactic he used was just as ingenious. Facing outside, he leaned forward and placed his coat over his left arm, which he somehow rested on the extremely narrow interior of the window. He hid his right arm under the coat as well. Then, like a trapdoor spider jumping out of a hole to snatch its prey, he used his right hand to quickly and discretely reach for whatever booty came within range. I watched him work at it for quite a while, marveling at his skill while keeping at just a safe enough distance.

When the novelty wore off, I turned to confront him.

Our eyes met. He looked away. When he looked back, I was still staring, a slight, almost imperceptible smile on my lips.

I wasn't mocking him. Neither was I trying to provoke him. I wasn't even angry. Perhaps being harassed and lied to felt more offensive than being the anonymous victim of a petty thief, which somehow felt less personal. It was an oddly intimate moment, a secret shared only by him and me, one that required no words.

He got the message and headed towards the middle of the bus.

Though I had let him off the hook, he wasn't so lucky shortly after when officials boarded looking for fare evaders. At least a fine was better than an arrest, I figured.

10 THE HONEYMOON

Before we caught the train back to Tangier, Sophie and I returned to the hotel to gather our things and rest for a while. When it turned out there was time for a quick dip in the pool, I left Sophie to her nap and ran downstairs.

As I went to place my towel on a chair, I noticed a half-full glass of lemonade.

"Is someone sitting here?" I asked the woman in the adjacent lounge chair. Several years my senior, she wore a tasteful sunhat and stylish frames, her bikini-clad body no stranger to the poolside. The table next to her was cluttered with glasses both empty and full, as well as a bottle of sunscreen and a paperback.

"Unfortunately," quipped the woman, with a laugh, shooting a wry glance at the man next to her. She had a British accent.

"What she means is yes. That lovely lady you see at the other end of the pool, who happens to be traveling with us," he said. A handsome thirty-something with neatly cropped hair and a slim, fit body, he, too, wore a pair of shades.

"And how did that happen again?" the woman taunted, letting out another laugh.

"I wish I could say," he shot back, perpetuating their inside joke.

"Actually, she's your compatriot—maybe you guys'll hit it off," the woman said, turning to me.

"At any rate, that lounge is free." The man motioned to the chair I'd asked about.

"Thanks," I said, draping my towel over it.

I didn't want to pry, but the couple seemed to be dying to give me the lowdown on their travel companion. Unable to resist, I lowered my voice and said, "So I guess your friend is sort of an unwanted guest?"

"Oh dear, is it that obvious?" joked the woman, whose name was Jane.

Out of nowhere, the American who was the unsuspecting subject of our conversation began shouting.

"Don't splash! Do not splash! I already told you not to splash!" She was furious.

The Moroccan boys who were the target of her ire just laughed, delighted to have gotten the reaction they wanted.

"Fais pas! Fais pas!" she attempted, as though the ordeal were nothing more than a linguistic misunderstanding.

When the boys began roughhousing again, thrashing water about in total disregard of her admonishment a moment before, she decided she'd had enough.

"I hate you! You're horrible! Both of you! I hope you drown!"

She floundered over to the ladder on the side of the pool. As she hastily pulled herself up, she slipped on the second rung, plunging backwards into the water with a giant splash.

Jane didn't even try to hold back a joyful cry of glee.

"Oh my god!" she laughed.

"Shhh! She's going to hear you!" scolded her friend, trying to suppress his own laughter. His name was Robert.

Even though I only knew part of the story, there was no fighting it. The sight of the demoralized prima donna tumbling into the water mid-tantrum was too much. I cracked up.

Her second attempt to get out of the pool having met with more success, the American lumbered towards us. Her wet, shoulder-length hair was as black as her one-piece bathing suit, which clung to undulating rolls of flesh. Dark hair flourished under her arms and trailed down her legs, all the more striking given her pasty skin.

The woman took advantage of her short stroll to reconstruct her fragile façade, dissimulating the true extent of the humiliation she'd just suffered at the hands of two teen-aged boys.

"My god, those boys were driving me crazy!" she exclaimed, her smile so forced it looked painful.

"They sure did enjoy razzing you, didn't they," said Robert.

"Yes they did! They most certainly did! Little brats!" she laughed just as unconvincingly. "Anyways, hi, I'm Gloria."

"I'm Matthew," I said, taking her wet hand into mine. It felt like greeting a seal.

"Oh! You're American, too."

"I am."

"Great! I think that's wonderful."

"Well, sure. I mean, yeah, I guess it is." I had no idea how I was supposed to respond.

"How do you like Morocco? I find it's a grueling place to travel alone as a woman."

"Alone? I thought you were traveling with—"

"Well, yes, Jane and Robert were nice enough to give me a ride from Marrakech. And we've been having so much fun I haven't even thought about striking off on my own again. It's so much easier traveling in a group, isn't it guys?"

"Sure is. That's why Robert and I came together," Jane remarked dryly, taking a drink.

"Anyway, I'm gonna head inside. I can't stand the heat if I can't cool off in the pool—which those little brats are obviously determined not to let me do! Nice meeting you. What room are you staying in? We should all get together later," she added, wrapping herself in a towel and putting on a pair of oversized sunglasses that recalled Hollywood's Golden Age. "I'm sure we'll see you later! Have a great day! Oh, and you guys, come by whenever you're ready to head out. Ta ta for now!"

"Ta ta!" mocked Jane once Gloria was out of earshot, adding a royal wave for full effect. "Do you think she thinks we say that? You guys, I mean you Americans, you don't say that do you? She says it all the time."

"Ta ta? No, I think she's probably just trying to be cute."

"You see! I told you!" Jane scolded Robert, playfully hitting him on the arm. "That pathetic creature is trying to be cute!"

"I never said they said that!" he protested.

"Oh yes you did. Last night you swore they did!"

"Last night I was drunk..."

"There you have it!"

"And so were you, so don't tell me you can be certain of anything that either of us said!"

"You see," Jane confided, turning back to me, "last night we had to drown our woes in an excessive indulgence of spirits."

"In other words, we got totally sloshed," clarified Robert, laughing again.

"So what's the story with—what was her name?—Gloria? She's gone now, don't keep me hanging!" I had to know.

"All we can tell you is how we came across her," Robert began.

"Ha!" contested Jane. "Hardly! We know a hell of a lot more than that! She hasn't stopped talking about herself—her boundless talents and endless knowledge and unbelievable experiences—since we picked her up."

"You picked her up?" I sensed we'd stumbled upon a good starting point.

"No, not exactly. That's not how I should have put it."

"The night before we were leaving our hotel in Marrakech," Robert explained, "the woman at the front desk found out we were renting a car to come north. She had just spent god-knows-how-long comforting this American girl, who'd been traveling by herself but had some sort of traumatic experience with a tour she was supposed to take."

"We still have no idea what the deal was with that,"

interjected Jane.

"Before we knew it the receptionist had called the American girl—Gloria—and asked her to come downstairs."

"If we had known what was about to happen, we would have bolted for the door and never looked back. God, I wish we had."

"Sadly, we didn't. The woman kept saying 'she's a nice girl, she's a very nice girl.'"

Jane took back over from Robert.

"So Gloria comes downstairs acting all meek and downtrodden, her cheeks streaked with tears that she demurely wipes away to elicit our sympathy."

"Which obviously worked," said Robert.

"It sure did. Then the receptionist tells her, 'These nice people are going to Fez by car. Maybe you can go with them.'"

"No way," I said.

"Oh yes. And since we didn't see it coming, neither one of us had time to think of a good excuse why we couldn't take her."

"We didn't have the nerve to just say outright that we preferred to spend our honeymoon alone," added Robert.

"What! Your honeymoon? You guys are on your honeymoon! Does Gloria know?"

"She most definitely does. You run out of things to talk about during a seven-hour drive, you know? It came up. Several times."

"We may have run out of things, but she didn't," Robert was quick to remind her.

"Oh god, she didn't shut up the whole time. She went on and on and on. My head hurts even thinking about it. The plan had been just to give her a ride, but she's such a leech—we can't get rid of her! She talks ad nauseam about being an independent woman who's seen and done it all, but it's a bunch of rubbish. She's clinging to us like a newborn to its mother!"

"Just tell her you want to spend the rest of your time alone. You're on your honeymoon! And it's not like you haven't done more than your fair share to help her."

"No doubt about that, but we couldn't keep her from staying at the same hotel," Robert rightly pointed out.

"We should have bribed the receptionist to say it was full," lamented Jane. "Yet another great idea come a little too late. That's why we're hoping you and she become fast friends. Don't you think it's time you did your part?"

"Actually," I said, glancing at the clock, "I've got to get going. My friend and I are headed back to Tangier."

"Oh my god, that's perfect!" Jane exclaimed. "Gloria was talking about Tangier this morning! You can take her with you!"

"No, no, that's okay," I said, rushing to collect my things. "She's all yours."

"But wait," Jane called out as I hastened inside. "She's a really nice girl!"

11 BIG TAM TAMS

A half an hour after leaving the honeymooning Brits stuck with the oblivious American, Sophie and I were at the train station, ready to head north. Not surprisingly, my thoughts turned to the last time I had left Fez. Then, rather than coming to the end of my travels, I wasn't even half-way through them. As our train pulled out of the station, I began sharing with Sophie what had ensued on my previous trip.

Since Peter the Australian and I were both headed to the Saharan sand dunes, we had decided to go together. Night had already fallen when we arrived at the small village that would be our jumping off point into the desert the next morning. Even before we got off the bus, we had to deal with the now-familiar hassle. As one young man tried to convince us to go along with him, another whispered in my ear that the first guy couldn't be trusted. We should trust him instead. He would take us to a very nice place.

We had already selected what we hoped would be a very nice place, a hotel located a short walk from the bus station. We hurriedly gathered our belongings, put up our defenses, and struck out in the direction of the hotel. An aggressive throng of men came at us with forced smiles, insistent offers, and unsolicited advice, outnumbering us by a scale of four or five to one. I said nothing, while Peter politely informed them we knew where we were going and didn't need any help.

Mere moments later, we came to realize something the Moroccans had known all along.

We did not, in fact, know where we were going.

It was possible the empty, unlit road with no buildings on either side led to our hotel. Eventually. Did we really want to find out? Did we really want to walk straight into the darkness, no indications we were headed the right way, followed by a belligerent group of men?

I quickly became overwhelmed. Too many questions, not enough information. Too many people coming at us from all sides. I couldn't think. I had to make it stop. I hung a 180 and made a beeline for the hotel next to the bus station. I didn't care how much it cost or how dirty it was or anything else about it, as long as it had a lock on the front door.

As soon as we stepped inside, the men behind us dispersed; all of them, that is, except one, who slipped in ahead of us.

"Good evening," a middle-aged man greeted us at the top of the stairs. I assumed he was the manager.

"He is not with us. He did not help us," I insisted, gesturing to the young man who had beat us inside.

"It's okay, there's no problem," the manager reassured us. "Here, let me take your things."

"You see, you should have trusted me," the young man admonished. As I contemplated his smug expression, it occurred to me there was little chance his disproportionately large head bore any correlation to a larger than usual brain.

It was also now clear that, just like all the others in the mob, he had been sent by the hotel to recruit guests. That being the case, I didn't trust either of them. Not yet.

"How much?" I asked, still holding onto my backpack.

The manager responded with a reasonable price. At the same time, two other young travelers came downstairs from the floor above. Reassured, we followed the manager to go check in.

As we sat down shortly after to omelettes and fries, the two guys from earlier came over to say hello.

"How's it going?" said one with an Australian accent. In his mid-twenties, his name was Gary, and he had the looks of someone who had been on the road for a very long time. Anemically thin, he had dark shoulder-length hair and a scraggly beard that hadn't been trimmed in weeks. His ragged t-shirt and baggy shorts probably hadn't been washed in almost as long.

His friend was more clean-cut. An American with short blond hair, a matching goatee, and a sturdy athletic build, while probably a little scruffier than he would have been under ordinary circumstances, he had hardly let himself go.

"A lot better now that we're inside," responded Peter.

"Yeah, we got here during the day, but it was just as bad," said the American, whose name was Jason.

We began chatting about our travels, comparing stories and sharing advice. Once Peter and I had devoured our meal, we all moved up to the roof. The proliferation of stars was stunning and, even though we couldn't see it, the presence of the desert was pervasive.

Gary had been in Morocco for over six weeks, whereas Jason had arrived only two weeks ago. They had met up in Ouarzazate, a town on the eastern side of the Atlas mountains, and had been traveling together ever since.

"I know this might sound totally random," Gary said to Peter when the conversation hit a lull, "but you look really familiar."

"You know," Peter confessed, "I've been sitting here thinking the same thing!"

After several near misses comparing their respective haunting grounds and social circles in Sydney, they hit the bull's-eye. They hadn't been imagining things. They had met briefly at a mutual acquaintance's party a few months earlier. Now they were meeting again thousands of miles away on the edge of the Sahara.

Small world.

Turning to look when we heard someone coming upstairs, we discovered Selim, the young Moroccan who had been part of the welcoming committee. Not bothering to wait for an invitation, he forced his way into our conversation. Oblivious to the cues of his guests, he was even bold enough to take charge of it, steering it towards his favorite subject: sex.

"Yeah man, my girlfriend and me, we did it six times in one night!" he boasted.

I diverted my gaze back up to the stars, Peter took another drink of mint tea, and Jason stifled an embarrassed laugh. Gary was the only one able to respond.

"Really? That's pretty impressive," he said with mock awe.

"Yeah," I added, "that must have been some night."

"It was amazing! You know, my girlfriend has big tam tams," Selim laughed, looking around to make sure we got the metaphor, which easily could have gone over our heads given its subtlety.

"Very big tam tams," he repeated, laughing harder while outlining in the air the voluptuous contours of his girlfriend's breasts. If his rendition were accurate, they did indeed seem to be of remarkable proportions.

"Cool," I said, while the rest of the guys seized the opportunity to let out suppressed laughter. "Does she know you call them that?"

"Know I call them that? Well, yeah. I guess."

The irony was lost on Selim.

"How old is your girlfriend?" Gary wondered.

"She is 15," Selim said, beaming.

Peter choked mid-drink, I failed to hold back a gasp, and Gary grinned from ear to ear.

"And you are..." Jason couldn't help but ask.

"I'm 29. Do you guys have girlfriends?"

We all shook our heads no, with the exception of Gary.

"I'm celibate," he confessed.

"Celibate? You mean, not married?" Selim asked. His French was better than his English, and he knew that *célibataire* meant "single" in French.

"No, I mean I don't have sex."

"Oh!" Selim made no effort to hide his astonishment. "Why not?"

"I choose not to."

It wasn't a notion Selim could even begin to fathom. As he struggled to make any sense of it at all—a man who actually chose not to have sex!—he was struck by the realization that maybe this wasn't a group of men with which he had much in common.

He practically ran back downstairs.

12 THE DESERT VISITOR

The four of us left the hotel first thing the next morning, stopping for breakfast at a nearby restaurant. We had agreed the night before to travel to Merzouga together, a small Bedouin settlement on the edge of the legendary Saharan sand dunes.

Finding transportation proved much more difficult than finding food. Already essentially in the middle of nowhere, there wasn't any public transport. We would have to hire a driver. Dividing in the hopes of conquering, Jason and I went off in one direction, while Peter and Gary went off in another.

A few minutes later, we reconvened to compare notes.

"How'd you guys do?" Jason asked.

"It was a little bizarre," Gary explained. "We got bounced from one guy to another. I guess there's some sort of pecking order, but no one wanted to explain it to us. It worked out though, because there's a guy with a van who says he's leaving in about a half an hour. His price seems pretty much in-line with what it says in the guidebook."

The price was considerably lower than what Jason and I were quoted, so it was a done deal.

The unpaved, pothole-laden road quickly disappeared as we

drove out of town. In its place there wasn't any road at all, at least not one I was able to discern. All I could make out were random tire tracks in the charred black crust of the desert floor. At first there were just a few, but many more followed. Coming and going in all directions, they crisscrossed in beguiling patterns, at times converging, only to diverge again soon after on their own phantom trajectories.

A respectful silence descended upon the van, disturbed only by the gentle voices of the two Moroccans in front. They had seen it all before, but the rest of us were mesmerized. A flat, barren desert extended to the horizon and beyond, a vast emptiness as expansive as the sky above.

There were no signs. We didn't see a single other vehicle. I was suddenly aware of having put our complete trust in the drivers. Ironic perhaps, given so many of our previous experiences. But I knew we were in good hands.

Somewhere well into the trip, contours began to appear in the terrain. The road became very rough. Before we knew it, the van was jostling around like a plane in turbulence. Peter spilled water down the front of his shirt.

A curious golden form eventually appeared on the horizon, a smooth silhouette arching softly into the sky. Though we were still at a distance, it seemed on a scale incongruous with its surroundings, dwarfing them. Its form and color, too, seemed strikingly out of place, inconceivably pure. It was followed by another, which gave way to more still.

The Saharan sand dunes.

Soon we were following their periphery, coming to the end of a grueling trip when at long last we got to Merzouga. A small number of buildings was scattered randomly about, dwellings and hotels run by the local Bedouins. The only sense of order came from a dusty, unpaved lane around which most of the buildings were loosely grouped.

We had arrived in the off season, and the village was nearly empty. After thanking our drivers, we split off into pairs to investigate our accommodation options. Peter and I immediately came upon a modest hotel built within the last year. Not only was it clean and economical, it was also completely vacant. We would have it all to ourselves.

A single-story adobe structure, like so much of the rest of the town, the hotel looked as though it could have risen right out of the sand. It had a whitewashed interior, and the main entrance opened onto a communal space where meals were had and stories exchanged. A short hallway led to five simple bedrooms and shared bathrooms.

The owner, a Bedouin with three little boys, was not only a good-natured, genuine host, but an amazing cook. For dinner he treated us to a fantastic *kalia*, a savory vegetable dish we all agreed was probably the best food any of us had tasted on our travels. We requested it again the next day.

Our bellies full, we lumbered up to the rooftop to enjoy the desert night. The stairs were on the outside of the building, made from the same baked earth as the rest of it. That proved true for the roof as well. I couldn't help but wonder if a heavy rainfall wouldn't wash the entire structure away.

Looking up at the cloudless nighttime sky, I had no doubt: I had never seen so many stars in my life. Ironic that ten minutes later I would see even more. Without warning, the few lights in the village all turned off at once. With absolutely nothing between us and it, the sky came that much more alive. It was mind-blowing.

When our fatigue finally got the better of us, we went back inside.

I was the first to see it.

Clinging to the wall at the end of the hall, in the faint light I made out a large form. About the size of a small rat, it didn't move.

"You guys, look!" I said, stopping dead in my tracks.

"What the hell is that?" asked Gary, moving in closer.

"Oh my god!" Peter exclaimed. "It's a bloody spider!"

"But it's got antennas," I observed.

All the same, Gary was right. Despite the feathery protrusions on its head, the creature had eight legs. It was an arachnid.

I had never seen such a large spider. It was larger than my fist, bigger than the tarantula I'd once seen crossing the road in Sequoia. Always a bit of an arachnophobe, I wasn't at all happy it had come inside to join us.

The spider darted up the wall, sending Gary reeling backwards.

"Jesus Christ!" he yelled.

"Shit!" said Jason, looking up. "How are we going to get it now?"

Not only was the roof high, but it was supported by rafters. Even if we could get up there, we had no way of knowing where the mutant beast—a rat-sized spider with feathery antennae?—was hiding.

"We're not," laughed Gary.

"All we can do is hope it doesn't come down in the middle of the night and crawl into our beds," Peter joked.

No one laughed.

13 THE DUNES

I woke up in a gritty pool of sweat mixed with sand.

Peter may have been an Australian, but he was no less wary of the spider than I was. So, despite being in the middle of the desert, we had closed the only window in our room and made sure there was no way the fugitive in the rafters could get through—never mind under—our door. By morning, the room was sweltering, and I felt as dehydrated as if I'd lost half my body weight overnight.

The plan for the day was to hike to the top of the largest dune in the area. If we wanted to get there and back without being burned alive by the desert sun, we had to get an early start.

On my way back from the bathroom, I knocked on Gary and Jason's door.

"Come in," answered Jason.

I opened the door, taken aback by what I saw. Gary was as pale as a ghost and drenched in sweat. Stripped down to his underwear, it seemed to take everything he had just to prop himself up in bed.

"Are you alright?" I asked.

"Oh sure, mate. Just got a case of the shits is all."

"Oh no, that sucks! I'm really sorry. I guess you're going to have to stay behind today?"

"He won't," Jason interjected. "I keep telling him we can do the climb tomorrow when he feels better, but he won't listen. I even offered to stay behind with him, but—"

"No way. To hell with it. I'm going with you guys and that's that. What if I die tomorrow? I don't want to die without having climbed Erg Chebbi—not after coming all this way and dealing with all the bullshit we had to deal with to get here!" he laughed.

He stood up to get ready, but suddenly had second thoughts.

"Actually, I think I need to head to the bathroom first."

He grabbed his roll of toilet paper and pushed me out of the way, making straight for the toilets across the hall.

"Is he going to be alright?" I asked Jason.

"I have no idea. But there's no way he should be hiking in the desert if he's got the runs."

"Well, it's his choice. Looks like it's going to be an interesting hike."

The sun was just coming up as we embarked upon our foray into the dunes, light and shadow at ever-changing odds in the undulations of the desert floor. The smaller dunes nearest us were darker than the larger ones further off. Tans, golds, and oranges, fiery reds. As the sun rose and our trek progressed, the sands would take on those and other colors, too, countless shades and hues.

In places the sand was rippled like the surface of a pond. In others it was littered with footprints of birds and animals now nowhere to be seen, most preferring the cool light of the moon to the scorching heat of the sun. As for our fellow humans, if anyone had been there the day before, the wind had effaced all traces of them.

Our own steps grew heavier with each we took. The sand gave way beneath our weight, hindering our gait and slowing our progress. It may have cooled overnight, but the desert floor was already warm, like embers that had never completely gone out.

The four of us wandered off on our own respective paths, the massive dune that was our destination looming overhead. The challenge the desert posed felt personal. Although at times the unforgiving landscape brought us together, inevitably it pushed us back apart. Each of us had to confront it on our own terms.

Occasionally the desert deceived us. From one side a dune might appear to show the way, only to drop off precipitously when we got to the top. When that happened, all we could do was turn around and look for another route.

The trek was hard enough for me, in good health. I couldn't imagine what it must have been like for Gary. Jason never strayed too far ahead of him, frequently looking over his shoulder to make sure his friend was doing alright.

Relieving himself before we left had taken the pressure off Gary's intestines. For a while. Now, not even halfway to the summit, the rumbling started again, weakening his entire body. Undeterred, he kept going, doing everything in his power to ignore the war being waged on his insides.

His indomitable resolve notwithstanding, he was fighting a losing battle.

"Don't look back!" he yelled.

"What?" asked Jason, turning to look and instantly regretting it.

Gary had dropped his pants.

"Don't look back! Just keep walking! I've got to go!"

As much as he abhorred the idea of defecating in the dunes, Gary had no choice.

"What's up?" Peter shouted to Jason.

"He's got to go! Don't look back!"

I couldn't hear what they were saying, and turned to find Gary's tragic image far below. Amidst astonishingly beautiful, unsullied waves of sand, a lone figure squatted, holding a roll of toilet paper. It was a peculiar, paradoxical sight.

It was also a hilarious one. Knowing I was too far away to be seen or heard, much like Gary himself, I couldn't hold back.

I burst into laughter, my own sides soon hurting almost as badly as his.

I was the first to arrive at the base of the biggest dune. Although I should have been covered in sweat, as I paused to catch my breath, I realized that in the dry heat my perspiration was evaporating as soon as it surfaced on my skin. Reminded of the need to stay hydrated, I took out my water bottle and looked behind me. Peter and Jason were both scaling the dune below, and Gary was on another not far behind.

I turned my attention back to my own ascent. A sheer wall of sand rising up before me, there was no easy way to the top. I would have to climb on all fours until I got to the lower end of the spine, which I could then follow up to the summit.

After another drink of water, I began scrambling towards the top. I didn't look up. I didn't want to know how far I had left to go. Instead, I concentrated on repeating my movements with as much economy as possible, my hands and feet sinking deep into the unstable sand over and over again. It was tough going, but I continued climbing, knowing that as long as I kept at it, I'd be to the crest in no time.

When I finally made it, I was astonished by what I saw. The smooth line demarcating where one side of the dune ended and the other began was extraordinarily precise. I didn't want to touch it. It pained me to think of defiling such perfection. I thought of the Buddhist monks who spend days meticulously rendering their sand mandalas, only to wipe them away in a dramatic testimony to impermanence. Sadly, if I wanted to see what was on the other side, I had no choice. I hoisted my weary body onto the spine, consoling myself that by morning the wind would erase all signs of my having been there.

One leg over each side of the crest, the soft sand now comforting ally as opposed to challenging adversary, I beheld an expanse of dunes so vast it defied the imagination. Calling it a "sea of sand" no longer seemed cliché; that was exactly what it was, its massive, successive golden waves rolling for as far as the eye could see.

When I got up to follow the spine to the summit, I looked down again at my friends.

"Almost there!" I hollered to Peter.

Jason was just behind him, but Gary had lost a lot of ground. I hoped we hadn't made a mistake by letting him come along.

The spine gradually sloped up towards the highest point of the dune. My walk felt like a victory march, and I savored each step as I continued to contemplate the staggering beauty visible in all directions. Even the bright blue sky was one of the most enthralling I had ever seen.

Peter joined me on the summit not long after.

"Wow," he said, taking a seat. "It's just incredible."

I turned to check on the others. Jason was just arriving at the crest a short distance below. Gary, on the other hand, had once again been waylaid.

"Uh oh, better just keep looking forward guys."

"Again?" asked Jason, his voice pained.

"No way!" Peter exclaimed.

Like witnesses to a train wreck, we couldn't help but look. It was every bit as tragic this time as it had been the first.

"The poor guy," said Peter.

"I told him not to come, I told him..." Jason lamented.

But then, out of nowhere, a laugh escaped him. He hadn't even seen it coming. He hadn't laughed before. Now though, seeing it all again, the vulgar anomaly in such stark contrast with the breathtaking beauty, the irony was too much, the vision too absurd. He couldn't help it.

Having essentially given voice to something Peter and I were thinking but too afraid to say, all three of us burst into laughter. My eyes were soon so full of tears I could no longer see out of them.

By the time we stopped, Gary had regained enough strength to begin the final ascent. Somehow he had come this far, and nothing was going to stop him from making it all the way to the top.

I just hoped we didn't to have to bury him there.

While we took in the spectacular panorama, slowly but surely Gary pushed himself higher and higher. Eventually, having given it everything he had, he threw one hand over the dune's spine, followed by the other. Then, with one final, decisive heave, he pulled his head over it, too.

Peter, Jason, and I all looked over in response to the grunt heralding Gary's arrival. His pathetic image even more comical than before, we all broke into another wave of laughter, rushing over to help him make the final jaunt to the summit.

There was no need to ask how he was feeling. He looked like someone who'd been stranded on a desert island for years. He was even thinner than when we had met two days before and as pale as a corpse, the hair both on top of his head and in his beard matted with an unsightly paste of sand and sweat. He was not in good shape.

But he had made it.

Once we finished celebrating Gary's arrival and calmed back down, we all fell silent. Even someone hopelessly out-of-touch with their feelings or woefully lacking any sense of something greater would have been hard-pressed not to feel a profound reverence. For creation. For our place in it. For its humbling, awe-inspiring mystery.

14 THE RETURN VISITOR

The routine that night was almost identical to the one before.

We ate dinner.

We spent a couple of hours talking under the stars.

We came inside to find a giant spider clinging to the wall.

We shouldn't have been surprised to see it again, but we were. When the owner's children were no less taken aback, I knew we had something truly special in our midst.

Someone found a bucket, which quickly made its way into Gary's hands. Despite his poor health, he was the only one up to the challenge. As if shitting his way up a forty-story dune hadn't been enough of a character-building experience for one day.

Slowly approaching the spider, he held the bucket out in front of him, the open end facing the wall.

The spider darted towards the ceiling.

Gary jumped back.

"What the hell!" he exclaimed, pausing to steady his nerves.

The spider hadn't gone all the way up to the rafters. There was still time. Gary took a deep breath to get up his courage. Then, casting his fears aside, he pounced. The bucket slammed against the wall. The spider was trapped.

The boys were beside themselves. They gasped and laughed

and said things we couldn't understand. One ran down the hall shouting, coming right back. The other two playfully pushed each other around. They had too much nervous energy. They had to do something with it.

Despite his partial victory, Gary was almost more miserable now than he had been before. He was sweating profusely, and there was a look of deadly serious concentration on his face. The spider may have been in the bucket, but the bucket was still open on the other end.

While the rest of us watched with baited breath—dreading one wrong move that might set the spider free—Gary lifted the edge of the bucket just enough for the hotel owner to slide a piece of cardboard between it and the wall. Gary tensed as he felt his captive moving around inside, no doubt startled by the unexpected intrusion and looking for a way out.

The boys went wild, the rest of us breathing a collective sigh of a relief. It was almost over. All that remained was for the hotel owner to take the bucket from Gary, paying extra special attention to keep the cardboard pressed against the top. Once that carefully orchestrated maneuver had been executed, the owner and his boys took a nighttime stroll far out into the desert, where they set the creature free.

We all slept a lot better that night.

15 WELCOME BACK AGAIN

Nine hours after leaving Fez, Sophie and I arrived in Tangier. Although we had walked to the train station the morning of our departure, since we were arriving late at night, this time we opted to get a cab—a ride that shouldn't have cost more than five or six dirhams, or less than a dollar.

Past experience having left me with a strong aversion to taxis—I'll always choose walking great distances over taking a cab in places I don't know—my stomach was wrapped in familiar knots as we came out of the station. Continuing past a couple of drivers who approached us, Sophie and I headed instead for the taxi at the head of the line. Surely that was only fair, after all. The fact the driver hadn't gotten out to hassle prospective customers only made him that much more attractive.

We opened the door and got in, surprised to discover a man sitting in the passenger seat. He was talking amicably with the driver, so we assumed they were friends.

We told the cabbie where we were going, making sure to distinguish our hotel by the port from one with a similar name in another part of town. The passenger up front also clarified for the driver, with whom we conducted the conversation in Spanish. Once everything was in order—including the meter, turned on and starting from the base rate—we set off on a trip that should have lasted all of ten or fifteen minutes.

Heading into town, Sophie and I shot each other confused looks as we passed one, then another opportunity to turn towards the port. There were even signs at both intersections, in the unlikely event the driver had forgotten how to get to the city's most defining landmark.

Before I could protest, Sophie moved forward in the seat, asking why we weren't going towards the port. The driver explained we had to drop off the other passenger first—a complete surprise, since neither Sophie nor I had realized he was a paying customer.

I recalled my experiences in Turkey, where there are types of shared taxis. Was there something comparable in Morocco? If so, was that what this was? I decided to ask.

That was it exactly, the driver confirmed. We were in a shared taxi.

Great. Except it still didn't feel right. Our taxi looked like all the rest, and at the train station we hadn't seen any others waiting to fill up with multiple customers. Having no way of knowing for sure and already in the cab, there wasn't much we could do.

Turning definitively away from the port and into the *nouvelle ville*, or "new" part of town, we drove along its main street, passing shops, cafés, and businesses familiar from our stay a couple of days earlier. Making another turn, when we got to the top of a hill we let out the passenger in front, who appeared to explain something as he paid the driver. The cabbie nodded dismissively, taking the man's money and turning his attention back to the road.

Although in reality everything had been all wrong from the moment we got into the cab, only now did we discover how wrong it truly was.

The previous passenger had paid for his trip. Yet the driver hadn't reset the meter. Once it was clear he wasn't going to do so of his own accord, I politely reminded him, "You're going to restart the meter, right?"

In a shocking setback sure to baffle the most experienced of neurolinguists, the driver suddenly forgot Spanish, a language he had spoken fluently until then. In its place, a series of grunts and gestures conveyed that, no, we would no longer be using the meter.

If it had been good enough for the Moroccan, it was good enough for us.

"Hold on, why aren't you going to use the meter?"

More grunts and gestures came in reply, this time all of them incomprehensible. It was heart-wrenching to watch someone who had been so charming and articulate only moments before lose all verbal communication skills from one instant to the next. If he hadn't managed to keep such an unfaltering eye on the road, I would have sworn we were witnessing him have a stroke.

"If we're not going to use the meter, then how much?" I demanded.

His condition having already advanced to the next stage, this time he didn't even respond. He was now a mere image of his former self.

"How much!" I demanded again, not bothering to hide my frustration. I knew the further we got down the hill, the more likely he'd feel justified in demanding payment, no matter how exorbitant the price—nor the fact we had never agreed to it.

When traffic forced us to a stop, the driver miraculously recovered his speech.

"Three thousand," he said, like a malicious child trying to see how much he can get away with.

"Three thousand!" Sophie and I exclaimed in unison. We already knew the fare should have been five or six dirhams. Five or six. Not hundred. Not thousand. At night it might have been a little more, but not six hundred times as much. In addition to being taken for a ride, once again we were being taken for idiots.

"In that case, we're leaving."

Turning to Sophie, I added, "Let's go!"

Grabbing our things—which we had been smart enough

not to let the driver put into the trunk—we jumped out of the car, adrenaline rushing as fight-or-flight kicked in and we hustled down a side street. We moved quickly but didn't run, reassured by the knowledge the driver couldn't leave his car in the middle of a traffic jam.

But then I looked over my shoulder.

His bravado knowing no bounds, the cabbie had in fact left his car behind. Running after us like an enraged bull down a street in Pamplona, I couldn't believe how fast his short, stubby legs carried his rotund body, which looked like it might burst at any moment.

"Run!" I shouted to Sophie, who was on the other side of the street.

How could this be happening? Why was the driver chasing us, as though we were the ones who had wronged him? Shouldn't it have been the other way around? Shouldn't he have been the one beating a hasty retreat, ideally from the police, once we'd reported him? How could he honestly feel we owed him something? It was mind-boggling.

Despite having no qualms about grinding traffic to a halt, there were still limits to how far the cabbie could stray from his vehicle. Soon he was forced to give up the chase and turn around, a discordant chorus of angry horns calling him back.

Though glad to see him abandon the pursuit, I felt little relief. He knew where we were going. And we weren't there yet.

"Come on!" I shouted to Sophie, encouraging her to pick up the pace.

When we came to a park separating the *nouvelle ville* from the medina, I felt another surge of anxiety. Situated on a well-lit slope, we may as well have been onstage. We were completely exposed to anyone in the plaza below or in the night market in front of the medina gateway, through which we had to pass to get to our hotel.

It was then that a little blue taxi tore into the plaza.

Despite the hundreds of them in Tangier, I knew right away this wasn't just any little blue taxi. My body tensed, once more seized by fight-or-flight. As I debated what to do, I noticed the driver had picked up more customers. For a split second, it seemed encouraging. He couldn't leave them to pick a fight with me, right?

Yet again I had underestimated him.

His car screeching to a halt in front of the medina archway, the driver jumped out and came running at me, stark, raving mad. I was mortified. I would have made a run for it right then and there, if it weren't for my misgivings about leaving Sophie on her own, the lone woman in a night market full of men. But when the driver got too close, I had no choice. I had to run.

I didn't go far, stopping as soon as I was out of his range, all the while desperately trying not to lose sight of Sophie. When the driver began yelling things in Arabic, I panicked even more, afraid of what lies he might be telling the quickly growing mob of men surrounding us.

"You didn't do anything for us! We don't owe you anything!" I yelled in French, so people would know there was more to the story.

I pushed my way back towards the center to be nearer to Sophie, only to be chased off a couple of more times. When I got a little too close on yet another attempt, the lunatic lunged at me as though I'd violated his only daughter. He was insane. Although I'd successfully avoided each of his previous attacks, this time he managed to grab my shoulder strap, swinging me around as though we were figure-skating partners. There was no way I was giving my bag up. With a determined tug I snapped it from his hands.

Our little spectacle having brought the night market to a standstill, we were now surrounded by about fifty men. I was living the chaotic mob scene from so many movies, and it was every bit as nightmarish as it had always looked on-screen. What were the men thinking? Who would they believe? What if they took sides with the cabbie? And where was Sophie? I couldn't lose sight of Sophie.

I was immensely relieved when some of the men held back the driver, allowing me to again retreat to the periphery. When

I looked back at the center, however, my stomach dropped to the floor.

Sophie was on her own in the middle of the mob, standing face-to-face with the madman.

Although being a woman hadn't exactly been advantageous for her thus far on our trip, Sophie figured that, in this particular instance, it would be. The driver wouldn't hit a girl.

Having no insight into what was going through her mind, I panicked even more, watching helplessly from what felt like miles away. All at once I imagined a million horrible things that could happen to her. Abduction. Torture. Rape. I had to get back to the center. I had to get her out of it.

Muscling past the men in front of me, once more I found myself at Sophie's side, yelling for her to come with me. Before she could react, the taxi driver went for me yet again, forcing me to the edge of the mob. I didn't know what to do. I couldn't leave her there. But every time I got anywhere near her, the driver came at me, forcing me to retreat.

As I was about to make another rescue attempt, I saw something peculiar. For just an instant the taxi driver paused from his histrionics, distracted by one of the men in the crowd. The man then handed him something.

What followed was even stranger. From one moment to the next the huge group began to disperse. What was happening? Where was everyone going? Where was Sophie? Now that people were going in all directions, my worst fear had come true.

I had lost her.

Frantic, I searched the disbanding crowd for some sign of Sophie. But she was nowhere to be found. My mind was racing and my body was trembling, as I struggled to keep it together.

"It's okay. It's okay," said a young man next to me, trying to calm me down.

"You should find your friend," added another, as though it hadn't occurred to me. Again all I could imagine was Sophie being dragged off to some dark alley and subjected to all sorts of unthinkable abuse, only to then be sold into the sex trade.

"That's exactly what I'm trying to do," I retorted. I didn't look at either man, for fear of missing what could be my last chance to see Sophie before she was taken away for good.

"She's over there," said another man, approaching me gently, like someone afraid of startling an abused animal.

Sure enough, there she was.

Apparently having escaped her would-be captors, Sophie had walked into the park. She was scanning the crowd for me, like I was for her.

Our eyes met. We ran to each other like long-lost lovers and embraced—but not for long. Turning towards the medina gate, we made a beeline for our hotel. It seemed we were out of danger but, given that neither of us knew why the driver had left, we couldn't be sure.

Unable to hold back, the whole way to the hotel we gave voice to our outrage. At the same time, we prayed the driver wouldn't be waiting for us when we got there. All we wanted was to be safe and sound inside, the rest of the world held securely at bay.

A few minutes later, we were back at the hotel.

The driver was nowhere to be found.

Still shaking from the trauma of the ordeal—our nerves not yet able to trust we were out of harm's way—Sophie and I broke out leftovers from the train ride and sat down to a late-night snack on our little balcony facing the bay.

The night we now looked out upon felt like an entirely different one from what we had left behind on the street. Other than the occasional rustling of a nearby palm, there was almost no movement or sound. Even the port parking lot, normally active at almost any hour, was quiet.

As we cracked pistachios and passed the water bottle back and forth, Sophie told me about her experience.

"I was confronting the taxi driver, and he suddenly only wanted 14 dirhams."

"Instead of 3000?" I asked incredulously.

"Yeah. A guy next to me explained the price of 3000 was in cents, not in whole dirhams."

"What? As if we were supposed to know that! Besides, 3000 cents still equals 30 dirhams, which is six times what the price should have been," I calculated. "He knew we didn't know the price was in cents—it was all part of the scam."

"Of course it was. That's why, when I was talking to him, he cut the price in half. He knew the original price was absurd, but he still wanted something. When I asked why he suddenly only wanted 14, he wouldn't say. I had a bill in my pocket I almost gave him, just so he'd leave us alone, but I didn't. I should have. It wasn't that much money."

"That's not the point! He was a liar and a thief, and we shouldn't have had to pay to shut him up. It might have been easier, but it wouldn't have been right."

"Well, right or wrong, it doesn't matter, since for whatever reason, he finally decided to leave."

I told Sophie about the exchange I'd witnessed between the driver and the man in the crowd.

"I really think he gave him money on our behalf," I concluded. It wasn't right that he had felt compelled to do so, but I was touched he had. "That stranger had our back."

Upon our return to the hotel, desperate for a shoulder to cry on, Sophie and I had wasted no time telling the men in reception about our ordeal. Not only did they adamantly confirm the driver should have used the meter and that the price he asked was exorbitant, they also urged us to go to the tourist police. Books were kept with photos of every driver in the city. If we could identify ours, his license would be revoked.

As much as I would have loved to see the shameless brute punished for what he had done not only to us but no doubt to other tourists as well, I hesitated. It was already well past midnight, and we were leaving first thing in the morning. What's more, despite the hotel manager's assurances to the contrary, all I could imagine was having to pay my way out of a Moroccan police station. I just wasn't up for it. I was too shell-shocked. I couldn't trust anyone so soon after what had happened.

"It hurts us, too," regretted the hotel manager, attempting one last time to convince me to go to the police. "It's a constant struggle."

I knew he was right, and I felt bad for letting him down. In the morning, a little shaken up but otherwise unharmed, we would be going back to Spain. He, on the other hand, along with countless others who made their living from tourism, would be suffering the consequences of not only what had happened to Sophie and me, but many other similar incidents throughout the country. They would be witness to few, if any, of them; but, they'd feel their impact, nowhere more so than in their pocketbooks.

16 THE MAD HATTER

As soon as we'd finished breakfast the next morning, Sophie and I headed to the port. We didn't bother to check the schedule. It didn't matter. We would be on the first ferry that would take us.

We happened to arrive shortly before the next one was about to leave. The ticket agent obligingly rushed to get us our tickets, motioning for us to carry our customs forms to the passport control booth. Neither Sophie nor I understood. When a man came forward to help explain, Sophie jumped with a start, grabbing her passport and wallet, wounds still fresh from the night before.

"I'm not a thief—I work here!" the man reassured her, almost as startled as she was and stepping back so she wouldn't feel threatened.

After finalizing some administrative formalities, the agent again insisted we get a move on.

"Where are our tickets?" demanded Sophie, fearing he was trying to pull some sort of scam and send us off without them.

"No, no, they're right there," I gestured, feeling bad for how the Moroccans must have interpreted her suspicions. Could they have any idea why she was so ill at ease? Or, not having experienced the challenges we had as tourists, did they simply think we were mean, suspicious people?

I thought back to a French couple I'd had the misfortune of traveling with on my previous trip, hoping Sophie and I weren't coming across as badly as they had.

At the time, I was still traveling with Peter, the Australian. Having just visited the Saharan sand dunes, our next destination was the Dades gorges. We hoped to take a long-distance taxi—faster and more comfortable than the bus, which wasn't leaving for another hour—but we needed someone to split the costs. Looking around, we saw a man and woman our age who appeared to be in the same situation. Before we knew it, we had all agreed to share a cab.

Two drivers had been waiting for our cue to begin negotiating. One approached and made an offer. While all of us thought it sounded a little high, our new travel companion, Jean-Luc, was outraged.

"Are you kidding!" he balked. "That's more than a Moroccan makes in an entire year!"

Not only was the driver stunned into silence, so were Jean-Luc's girlfriend, Hélène, and I. Peter was spared the horror of the arrogant gaffe, since the negotiations were taking place in French.

Regaining his composure, the driver muttered something in Arabic and stormed back to his car.

Before I could reconsider traveling with the couple, two more drivers approached. We negotiated an acceptable price with one, and mere minutes later we were off.

Jean-Luc and Hélène lived in Paris. They had been traveling a little over a week and were planning on staying for another. Unassuming and polite, she was attractive in a pleasant, unremarkable way. She wore her dark blond hair pulled back because of the heat, her skin showing little signs of having seen the Moroccan sun. He was taller than she was with a small paunch, thin arms, and hairy, tree-trunk legs. Although he took pride in his appearance—his thick hair perfectly coiffed in defiance of the elements—his ill-fitting shorts, polo with upturned collar, and leather loafers seemed questionable choices. Designer frames protected dark beady eyes, and his head was perpetually cocked in suspicion and disdain.

The trip was intensely hot, all the more so because the taxi lacked air conditioning. The fact it was darting like a bullet across the desert plain made little difference, sweltering heat streaming in through the vents. At times the stark, rocky landscape was black, the earth charred to the point of cracking, seemingly scorched beyond any possibility of supporting life.

Occasionally we came upon a town, our vehicle forced to slow down as it meandered through busy streets. Whenever we did, conversation stopped, as we all paused to look out the window, fascinated to see people living in realities so different from our own. Inevitably the townspeople were as curious about us as we were about them, straining to catch a glimpse of the foreigners passing through their midst.

After a few hours on the road, we arrived at a hotel recommended in one of our guidebooks. The reception was empty, although we heard Arabic music emanating from somewhere deep within the building.

We called out. Nothing. Hélène walked ahead, following a corridor that led to a large sitting area. Glass doors opened onto a beautiful view of the mountain behind the hotel and a terrace abutting a small creek, gurgling at its feet.

"I'm surprised there's so much water," Hélène remarked, crouching down. After so much time in the bone-dry desert, it wasn't enough to merely look at the water. She needed to touch it, to feel its cool caress.

"Madame!" came a voice from behind us, alarmed.

Hélène froze, turning to find a handsome Moroccan in his mid-20s standing in the doorway.

"I'm so sorry," he said, his initial expression of concern giving way to a polite smile. "It's just that...well, let me show you."

He picked up a palm leaf and stirred the water, disturbing a multitude of nearly formless black creatures lurking in the creek-bed vegetation.

"Leeches," I observed with disgust.

"Leeches?" asked Hélène, not familiar with the word in English.

"Des sangsues," translated the young man.

"Mais non! C'est dégueulasse!" Hélène exclaimed in disgust.

Introductions took place and before long we were situated in two comfortable, spacious rooms overlooking the mountains.

The next day we awoke to a familiar pitter patter. It seemed out of place and, as I slowly came to, I wondered if I was hearing right. Walking to the window, I confirmed that I was: it was raining. Puddles on the ground and a swollen creek suggested it had been for quite a while.

Fortunately, before breakfast came to an end, so had the precipitation. Relieved our excursion to the gorges wasn't getting rained out, we set off, Jean-Luc immediately lodging his first complaint of the day: he had lost his hat. His extra-sensitive eyes were now extra vulnerable to the sun's blinding rays. Except he was wearing sunglasses. Why was the hat so important for his eyes? I decided not to ask.

The trailhead was a twenty-minute stroll from the hotel. Soon we were walking through a spartan terrain of reddish rock accented by colorful wildflowers. Jean-Luc initially took the lead, but quickly grew tired of the bothersome insects alongside the trail. Every time we approached a bush, they took flight with an alarming buzz. Hélène moved to the head of the line, untroubled by the harmless bugs.

Ascending a steep ravine, its rough, striated walls thrust upwards by an ancient seismic upheaval, we came out onto a ridge dividing two mountain flanks. Wide but steep, it afforded spectacular views of an arid valley far below. A river winded along the valley floor, flanked by the only green in sight other than occasional bushes defying the odds on the mountainside, surviving with almost no water. The dramatic landscape reminded me of the Grand Canyon, while for Peter it called to mind a similar region in Australia. Jean-Luc and Hélène had never seen anything like it.

On our way back to the hotel, we came upon a roadside inn we'd seen on the way to the trail. Everyone hungry from the hike, we decided to stop for lunch.

A portly man in his 50s named Ahmed greeted us. Jovial and curious, rather than get right down to business, Ahmed wanted to chat. He was so eager to talk, in fact, I couldn't help but wonder how long it had been since he'd had any human interaction.

He explained that the region hadn't seen any precipitation for months and that a thunderstorm (I hadn't heard the thunder, but Peter had) this time of year was very unusual. When we told him where we had hiked, he regretted to inform us we hadn't made it to the actual Dades gorges. We'd turned off too early and explored another area that, though beautiful in its own right, was nothing in comparison.

Just when we thought he was going for the menus, Ahmed got out his guest books.

"I have many, many guests from all over the world," he explained, "and I have them all sign my book."

There were four or five, each full of photographs and long, glowing tributes to the incomparable hospitality each and every guest had experienced at Ahmed's roadside inn.

The kudos went on and on, page after page. I began to wonder if we'd have to get through them all before we could eat. Ahmed was so enthusiastic about sharing, I didn't dare ask, for fear of hurting his feelings.

Jean-Luc had no such qualms.

"Are we going to eat?" he asked point blank.

"Ah oui! Bien sûr!" Ahmed exclaimed, as though snapped out of a stupor. "I almost forgot! What would you like?"

His offerings were limited, consisting exclusively of vegetable dishes.

"I can make you a kebab," he added almost by way of apology, "but I would have to walk a half an hour to town to get meat."

Peter shot me a look asking if he'd heard right. Had Ahmed

really just offered to walk half an hour to get meat? He couldn't drive, because of a mudslide further down the road.

"I'll have the tajine," I said. By now I was ready to eat just about anything. I hoped my making a quick decision would prompt the others to do the same.

Peter followed suit, also ordering the tajine. Hélène wasn't sure yet, and Jean-Luc needed more information.

"You said you had kebab?" he asked.

My jaw dropped. Was it possible Jean-Luc had somehow failed to hear Ahmed say he'd have to walk half an hour to get meat?

Ahmed was no less taken aback, though he tried not to let it show. Pausing to regroup, he smiled patiently before lowering his voice and repeating—almost gravely, as though broaching a delicate subject—what would be required of him to prepare a kebab.

Jean-Luc didn't care. Rather than back down, he continued debating whether or not to order the meat dish. Hélène intervened, gently trying to persuade him that a vegetable one would be preferable. He, however, was defiant. He would choose what he wanted on his own.

After exhaustive deliberations, Jean-Luc came to a decision.

He had settled on an omelette.

"Not again," he muttered to himself.

Ahmed looked as relieved as if he'd just passed a kidney stone, disappearing to the kitchen before Jean-Luc had any second thoughts.

Refusing to let it go, Jean-Luc explained to Hélène that getting the meat wouldn't have been that big a deal. No doubt Ahmed was exaggerating, and he would have just sent "one of the boys". Exactly which boy Ahmed would have sent was hard to say, since we had neither seen nor heard another soul since our arrival.

After leaving our marks in the annals of Ahmed's history, we returned to the hotel, gathered our belongings, and prepared for the next leg of our journey.

Finding transportation proved problematic. The first

minibus that passed was heading up the mountain and wouldn't be returning for at least an hour. The second was headed in the right direction but was already filled beyond capacity, even by local standards.

Twenty minutes later, a white minibus rounded the curve up the road, pausing just long enough for the four of us to pile in. It was already half full.

Scarcely had we gotten settled, than Jean-Luc had another outburst.

"Mon chapeau!"

"What's that?" asked Hélène, as taken by surprise as the rest of us.

"My hat!" he cried again, still in French, as out of control as a child throwing a tantrum.

All eyes followed his finger, pointed at a young Moroccan man in the passenger seat up front.

Once again Hélène tried to calm down her hysterical partner. He would have nothing of it. The Moroccan had his hat, and he was going to get it back. No matter what.

The hat in question was a red baseball cap—a cheap knock-off of a popular European brand. They were everywhere. How could Jean-Luc be so sure this particular one was his? It wasn't as if the Moroccan had stayed at our hotel or shared our cab the day before. The chances he would have come across Jean-Luc's hat were about as good as the chances of Jean-Luc exhibiting a moment of humility.

All eyes on him, the accused said nothing. He glanced at the driver, then diverted his gaze outside, as though oblivious to the mad Frenchman.

"Are you going to give me my hat?" demanded Jean-Luc, refusing to back down.

The man still said nothing. Hélène pleaded for Jean-Luc to stop. He, however, was only more convinced with each passing moment of the legitimacy and valor of his crusade.

As if he hadn't already gone too far, he went a step further.

"When I get back to France, I'm going to tell all the French people that Moroccans are thieves! Is that what you want me to tell them? Huh?" he ranted.

I was embarrassed. I was angry. I cursed the moment we had agreed to share a cab.

The minibus stopped to pick up a couple of more passengers, who stuffed themselves in back next to Hélène and Jean-Luc. Not missing a beat, Jean-Luc explained to the newcomers how he'd been wronged not only by the man in front, but countless other Moroccans throughout his trip. It made no sense. Why was he looking for sympathy from the very people he was insulting? Stranger still, why was he getting it?

It was the same scenario I would observe later when the self-destructive, manipulative old man in Tangier turned a whole crowd against the café worker. Didn't these people see any reason to question the raving Frenchman's story? Weren't they at all offended by his accusations and insults about their compatriots?

Jean-Luc continued throwing his fit, the Moroccans who had befriended him up at arms at the cruel, unjust fate he'd suffered in their country. Still, no matter how loud he complained, no matter how offensive his allegations or threats, the man up front refused to acknowledge his spectacle.

We arrived at our destination, scores of other minibuses and taxis congregated at what was essentially a regional transit hub. No sooner was the door thrown open than Peter and I bolted for a shady corner on the other side of the sea of vehicles. We wanted no part of Jean-Luc's grand finale.

That didn't mean, however, we weren't going to watch it.

From our vantage point, we couldn't hear what was said. We saw Jean-Luc approach the Moroccan wearing "his" hat and gesture aggressively, making a scene that began to draw in other drivers and passers-by. That we had expected. What we hadn't expected was what came next.

Without a word, the Moroccan handed Jean-Luc the hat and walked away.

While Peter and I questioned whether we'd seen correctly, Jean-Luc practically jumped up and down with glee, vindicated by his perceived victory. But that wasn't what it looked like from our perspective. To us it seemed much more likely the unjustly accused Moroccan had taken the higher ground, giving the spoiled Frenchman the hat like he might have given a bratty child their toy.

By the time Jean-Luc and Hélène were ready to discuss transportation options, Peter and I were already on our way out of town.

17 THE HUMBLE EGOTIST

Morocco is a beautiful country with an incredible amount to offer, from the fascinating Imperial Cities to the spectacular Rif mountains to the awe-inspiring Saharan sand dunes.

Perhaps that sounds strange for me to say after some of the stories I've told, but my words are sincere. It's because I found the country so captivating, after all, that I was willing to return despite the challenges encountered on my first trip. I wouldn't have returned if I didn't think—or at least hope—it would be worthwhile. I wanted to let bygones be bygones and give Morocco a second chance. I was living so close, there could have easily been not just one return trip but many. I was even thinking about studying Arabic there. I had more than enough reasons to want my second trip to Morocco to go well.

Unfortunately, although things initially went better than expected, at the end of my four-day trip with Sophie, I felt like someone who had left behind an abusive relationship only to go back and learn the same lessons all over again.

Walking out of our hotel the morning after the altercation with the cab driver, I didn't want to talk to anyone. I was still raw. I just wanted to be left alone and catch my boat. When a storekeeper insisted on inviting us into his shop as we walked down to the port, I said nothing.

"Egotist," he sneered.

I wanted so badly to turn around and describe for him in vivid detail every misadventure I'd experienced in his country. I wanted to explain that, despite not wanting to chat with him that morning—which, after all, was merely a pretext for being drawn into his store to be pressured into buying something—I actually appreciated he was just trying to make a living. I wanted to let him know that, rather than an egotist, I was a physically and emotionally exhausted traveler who had given his country a good-faith second chance. Although it hadn't gone as well as I had hoped, I wished him and his fellow Moroccans all the best.

ABOUT THE AUTHOR

A longtime resident of San Francisco, Matthew Félix has also lived in Spain, France, and Turkey. Adventure, spirituality, and humor infuse his work, which often draws on his time living in the Mediterranean, as well as his travels in over fifty countries.

matthewfelix.com

Debut novel out now

A Voice Beyond Reason

"Beautifully Written, Full of Important Truths"
- Sandra, Vine Voice

In his mountaintop village in southern Spain, Pablo's entire life seems planned out for him. When family tragedy catapults him into an unconventional journey of self-discovery, the profound transformation of his inner world leads to dramatic changes on the outside as well.